# Glimpses
# *of* Heaven

# Glimpses *of* Heaven

*True Stories of Hope and Peace*
*at the End of Life's Journey*

## Trudy Harris, RN

© 2008 by Trudy Harris

Published by Revell
a division of Baker Publishing Group
PO Box 6287, Grand Rapids, MI 49516-6287
www.revellbooks.com

Spire edition published 2021
ISBN 978-0-8007-3956-0

Printed in the United States of America

21   22   23   24   25   26   27       7   6   5   4   3   2   1

To all those whom God sent to our care
and who taught us life's lessons along the way.

# Contents

# *Foreword*

I've often said that "heaven is a real place." Not a concept, not an idea—but a "real place."

Who better to remind us of this than a hospice nurse who witnessed glimpses of heaven countless times through the lives and deaths of her patients. Trudy Harris, through the work of her heart and her hands, has served as a caring facilitator for so many through the twilight of their time on earth. I'm not sure I could serve as faithfully or as fearlessly in the role to which God called her.

As a hospice nurse, Trudy has seen and heard things that cannot be explained in human terms. In these spiritual moments, between earthly and eternal life, she has seen God at work over and over again.

You will find comfort in the story of Zach, a three-year-old boy who faced death with love and peace. You'll get a glimpse of heaven through the story of Lenora, a mother in midlife who saw an angel standing by her bed, ready to take her home. And you'll witness God's graciousness and mercy, as a calloused elderly man named Johnny receives a message from a God who longs to redeem him before he breathes his last breath.

If you believe in God, your faith will be strengthened and renewed. If you are skeptical or simply curious about what happens when we die, these stories will give you food for thought. In these pages you will find insights into what happens in the final hours and days of our time here on earth.

This remarkable collection of true end-of-life stories offers comfort, hope, and peace for the next stage of life's journey. Thank you, Trudy, for reminding us all that heaven is a real place. Yours is a book I will heartily recommend to many who have lost or are losing a loved one, and to anyone who longs to know more about the reality of our heavenly home.

Until I see you at the gate,

Don Piper

# Introduction

Many years ago, I was visiting a terminally ill patient at his home in the middle of the night. As I entered his room, he smiled and, pointing to the window nearest his bed, said to me, "There's an angel at my window, Trudy. Can you see him?" It was more than evident to me that Pat was actively dying and had very little time left, maybe an hour or so. He was peaceful and unafraid but awestruck by what he was seeing. I explained to him that God was preparing to take him home very soon, and He was letting him have a glimpse of heaven before going in. He smiled knowingly, nodding his head in agreement, and seemed totally at peace with that thought. Since he lived alone, I promised to stay with him until he was taken there safely by the angel who was watching over him now. Sitting on the floor next to his bed, I held his hand for less than an hour until he died.

Over many years, family members, friends, and patients in my care have shared with me their very personal experiences of dying. Their experiences are as varied and unique as the persons themselves, and are shared with an openness and confidence that can only be explained by their anticipated and imminent meeting with God. He speaks to their spirits in a way no one else ever has as He prepares to call them home. No one has to tell them they are dying; they know and recognize His voice. They have developed what I call "spiritual eyes and ears" and seem to see and understand things in a way we cannot. The experiences are unique to the persons themselves but share a common theme of enlightenment, love, and acceptance at the end of life. They give us glimpses into a world none of us has yet seen but one day will. Each person seems to receive exactly what he or she needs to see and hear in order to die peacefully and well.

As the physical body declines, the spiritual self becomes apparent and seems to yearn in a real and tangible way for someone or something greater than itself. This appears to be a very natural movement on the part of the dying person and is expressed in a myriad of ways. People who are about to die are very generous in sharing their experiences if they feel you will be open to hearing them. They tell you about their experiences as they are living them and seem to want to help you understand the simplicity of it all.

This temporary tent, which is our body, is changing, and no one knows this better than the person who is dying. If you sit quietly and listen to them, both their questions and their insights, they will invite you to share in this next, awesome step in life's journey. There is nothing left to hide, nothing to gain, and nothing to prove or lose, thus making the sharing totally pure. And when you enter into the wonderment of these blessed experiences with them, you yourself will grow.

Visions of those who have gone before them, angels, beautiful music, and personally comforting experiences permeate the minds and hearts of those who are dying. The imprints of their shared experiences are left with us to ponder and more importantly to provide a platform for our own lives. This book does not attempt to define or provide meaning to what people see and hear. Rather it offers a portrait of what we might expect when our time inevitably comes and demystifies death as only first-person accounts can do.

When patients and friends who were dying would say to me, "Today is my day" or "I saw my name on the marker" or "I heard them call my name" or "My son is here with me now; he said it's time to go," at first I simply did not understand. When many others told me about seeing angels in their rooms, being visited by loved ones who had died before them, or hearing beautiful choirs or smelling fragrant flowers when there were none around, I assumed it was the result of the medications they were taking or possibly dehydration. Surely the visions could not be real. But when others who were dying and not on medication and not dehydrated were saying the same things, I started to listen, really listen.

When they spoke of angels, which many did, the angels were always described as more beautiful than they had ever imagined, eight feet tall, male, and wearing a white for which there is no word. "Luminescent" is what each one said, like nothing they had ever seen before. The music they spoke of was far more exquisite than any symphony they had ever heard, and over and over again they mentioned colors that they said were too beautiful to describe.

I have the feeling that people do not die at the exact minute or hour that we say they do. In some inexplicable way that we do not yet understand, they seem to travel back and forth from this world to the next, developing the insights God wants them to have on this, their final journey back to the Father who created them.

Friends of mine who are physicians and nurses have often suggested to me that hearing about and understanding the experiences of terminally ill and dying patients would be of great comfort to everyone in the medical profession. Those who have allowed themselves the luxury of being present with patients as they are dying come away realizing in a whole new way that there is only one Divine Physician, and it is He alone who sets the timetables of our lives.

A patient who was afraid to die lying flat on his back asked me to hold him in a sitting position as he was dying. Moments before he died he said to me, "Trudy, there is no such thing as time. Dying is like walking from the living room into the dining room, there are no beginnings or endings." The words he spoke were in response to my looking at my watch as I foolishly counted his respirations, and he smiled a very patient smile as he said it. Then he closed his eyes and died. There are so many new insights, so many opportunities to think and understand in a whole new way when seeing from the perspective of the patient who is moments away from entering heaven. There are so many important lessons people are trying to teach us moments before they die. We had better listen. We are standing on holy ground during these moments, and we dare not miss one of them.

Trudy Harris

*The names, diagnoses, and histories of those portrayed here have been changed to protect the privacy of those in my care. In those instances where families have asked me to use the real names of their loved ones, I have done so.*

# Daddy

*"Martin said it's time to go."*

My dad was a big, loving Irishman of sixty-eight years who had lived and loved well. "Don't wait too long to come and see me," he said. "I haven't much time left." I had called Dad from the South Carolina beach where I was vacationing with my family. It was Father's Day, June 1973. Dad had broken a rib while picking up a statue on the outside of their house and moving it for my mother. He was in a great deal of pain and didn't know why. Tests over the next four weeks showed a diagnosis of multiple myeloma with widespread disease to the bone. CAT scans reflected a large tumor on the left kidney as well. The doctors said Dad had less than one year to live, and without surgery he could have less time than that, with the possibility of hemorrhaging to death. Time was very short, and no one knew it better than Dad.

Dad had been a wonderful father to his four daughters, who now took turns staying with Mom and helping with the day-to-day needs they shared. He had a great zest for life, endless Irish humor, and a love for my mother that could not be measured. She was his main concern in life, always had been, always would be. Even now as he was dying, she continued to be his primary focus.

One day, as four doctors circled his hospital bed with multiple ideas as to how to handle his care, he turned to me and said, "Can they make me better, honey?"

"No, Dad," I said. "I don't think so."

"Then take me home now," he said with such authority as to leave no doubt in anyone's mind as to what he wanted. We did exactly that.

Dad was a great talker all his life, and he loved to share his ideas and thoughts and loved hearing yours. As a labor leader and union negotiator in New York City, he could see and hear both sides of an argument and loved to play the role of bringing people and their ideas together. He often pondered about business friends and acquaintances and those with whom he had worked who had lived less than good lives and had gotten away with it. He wondered with a chuckle about the chance of some of them getting box seats in heaven while he was in the bleachers. He was never judgmental but had great humor and loved thinking out loud about all the possibilities.

He loved retelling Jesus's story about the landowner who had invited workers into his vineyard at different times of the day and paid them all equally at the end of the day. As a union organizer who was always concerned with a fair day's wage for a fair day's work, Dad would question Jesus's thinking and suggest that a good union could have made a difference for them. He said all this in jest, of course, figuring that Jesus, in His infinite mercy, had His own way of handling things, which in turn was a good lesson for us all. His lifelong musings were the foundation of our very early learning, and he had a unique and wonderful way of telling the stories, which would ultimately play a major role in who each of his children became.

One morning, just days before Dad died, I was giving him a nice shave. He looked into the mirror and said to me, "I don't look like I'm dying, do I, honey?"

"No, Dad, you really don't," I said.

"I really don't mind dying, you know. I'm ready. I just hate leaving Mommy. Don't let anyone ever hurt her, OK? She's just too good for anyone to upset her or make her feel sad." Dad's concern had always been for others: those who might be vulnerable, those who were less fortunate, those who were alone, and those who could not help themselves. Especially now, he wanted to be sure that the great love of his life would be protected and safe and that no harm would come to her. It was so like him.

Although I didn't realize it fully at the time, Dad was really talking with me about his impending death. His time was very close, and like all people who are about to transition into a new life, which we call death, he knew it, he felt it; no one had to tell him. God was preparing him Himself. The Holy Spirit, to whom Dad had turned throughout his life for guidance and direction, was playing a major role in his understanding and insight now. He seemed so at peace with it all, as if with an old friend who understood him well and with whom he was very comfortable. It was awesome to watch.

"I didn't always like you, you know," I said to him one day while we were alone. "But I always loved you. I especially loved you when you bucked me, stood your ground, and told me the truth, whether I wanted to hear it or not."

"You didn't like me because you were just like me," he said with a big smile. We had butted heads often because we were so alike, often coming to the same understanding of truth but at different times and in different ways. "You always know just what I need before I have to ask," he said in response to my changing the pillow at his feet.

Dad had a way of letting you know how important you were to him and what he thought of you with just a smile or simple pat. *What a good and truthful man he is,* I thought. *This is the very best it can be. My father is leaving us to go on to the God he has always loved and followed with the same certainty, confidence, and peace he exhibited all his life . . . how natural.*

Then it was Maggie's turn to be with Dad. She was the "little one" he always felt a need to protect. She had an impish nature, which caused her to test the envelope a lot growing up. Dad was always there to happily bail her out of her young antics. It was now her turn to explain things to him, to make him laugh, and to show him who she had become because of him. The day he died, Dad greeted her in the morning, saying, "Maggie, Martin said it's time to go now." Dad was referring to Martin Kyne, his friend of forty years who had died less than a year before. Dad was very peaceful when he told her that he had seen Martin. He said it so calmly as though it was just understood. He was letting her know he was ready to die. He gifted his daughters, even now as he was dying, in the ways he knew would be most comforting for each of them. He knew each of us well, so it came naturally for him.

Maureen, the eldest daughter, lived with Mom and Dad and had a work ethic that he admired greatly. "You work so hard all the time but you never complain," he would often say to her. They both felt strongly about hard work and principle, and she said many times that, for her, Dad represented the true living gospel of Jesus Christ. "He didn't just talk about it," she would say. "He lived it every day in all the things he did for others."

Anne, as the youngest, was in constant attendance with both Mom and Dad, meeting their every need. She was always the one who tried to fix things, to make everything right, and she was doing this now in her own special and gentle way, wordlessly. Dad especially loved having his "Annie Fresh Eggs" around him now, reflecting the sweet soul she had always been growing up.

Dad thought about others first throughout his life; and even now he continued to do the same, putting others at ease, their well-being uppermost in his mind. The lessons he taught me during this period of time prepared me for a future of serving the needs of the dying through hospice care in a way I could never have known otherwise. The gentleness and naturalness of his passing demystified death for me and allowed me to see God's gentle and constant hand on the souls of His children as He prepares to take them back home to Himself. I will be forever grateful to my dad for his strength of character, constant love, and faith in me and for the great love he exhibited all his life.

Only six weeks after his original diagnosis, Dad was curled up in bed with Mom beside him, quietly resting. Turning to her he said, "I love you, Peggy," and taking one last, gentle breath he traveled from this world's experience into his eternal reward. He was with the love of his life until the end, and his leaving, though very sad, was a gentle and natural experience. It was covered by a faith nurtured through the ups and downs of spiritual growth by a God who was always with him.

Dad walked and talked with God throughout his life, searching for Him in the hard places of personal growth and refinement. He reflected Him in the compassionate ways he attended to those struggling to make a dignified living for their families; in the ways he cared for his mother and sisters and brother when his own dad died so young; in the way he cherished and respected Mom all her life; and in the many ways he nurtured his four daughters into womanhood.

He depended on God's direction for everything and now could simply turn himself over to the God whom he knew and trusted so completely. He taught us so many things while he was living and even more when he was dying. He was an unforgettable man.

# Mary Anne

*"Why did God let me live longer
than the doctors said I would?"*

Mary Anne, a wealthy investment broker, married with no children, came to my door one day. She lived in a world of social activity, wealth, and country clubs, a world that was very different from mine. "I understand your father died recently," she stated as she pushed past me and seated herself in my family room early one morning. "I didn't know what to bring you," she said, handing me a brass door knocker wrapped in tissue paper. "So I got you this." Nothing sat well with me that day in regard to Mary Anne. I didn't understand the gift at all and did not want to, and only later did I realize the symbolism involved with the "knock at the door."

I have to confess: I didn't like Mary Anne very much. She was a strong, outspoken businesswoman, and I was sure we had nothing in common. Why was she here?

"I'd like to hear about your dad's death," she said. "How it was, what he said, how he died. I want to know all about it."

Her prodding questions made me both uncomfortable and angry. In spite of my feelings, I somehow knew deep inside myself that this was the beginning of something that I did not yet understand, something I was to experience and from which I was to learn. What the lesson was to be, I had no idea. It seemed that God's plan for Mary Anne and for the things to come was just unfolding. Needless to say, over a period of time and out of my control, we became very good friends. God taught each of us what He wanted us to know through the other.

She came to visit often, always asking questions about life and its meaning and purpose. She asked about God and about Jesus. "Where is it written? How do you know, how do you find Him?" Mary Anne had an unquenchable thirst and could barely get the questions out fast enough. She needed to learn about many things, and she seemed to be in a hurry.

During a visit one day she told me that she had inoperable cancer, which had been diagnosed just days before my dad died. She wanted to be close to someone who had experienced death firsthand, and she wanted to know everything she could about what happened and why. It was the businesswoman in her that made Mary Anne want to have a plan and to understand as much as she possibly could. It was God's invisible hand putting her together with those who would walk this way with her, experience her struggle, learn from her, and be there for her when she found Him. It was awesome and humbling to be part of it.

Mary Anne's diagnosis was deadly. Her cancer, first discovered in the breast, had spread rapidly to both lungs and the lining of her chest wall. Her prognosis was three to four months. She lived for two and a half years. What exciting, searching, joyful, and difficult years they were! It was more than evident to me from the start that God loved Mary Anne dearly and wanted her to know Him well. Thus began her long and wonderful journey. Visiting her was like being in a church sanctuary. You wanted to take your shoes off because you felt as though you were on holy ground. The presence of grace was always evident as Mary Anne journeyed toward God, experiencing Him in many, many ways.

My prayer for Mary Anne over this long period of time had been, "Lord, put Your arms around her, hold her in Your tender loving care, and help her to know she is safe with You." One day while I was visiting, Mary Anne explained the first of many spiritual experiences she would eventually have. "I was not asleep," she said to me very pointedly. "I was awake, and He came to me here in my room. He put His arms around me, and I felt so safe and warm."

"That was Jesus," I said to her.

"No, it wasn't, Trudy, it was you," she said with a lovely smile.

*What does it mean?* I wondered. Is this how God visits with His children, through fragile and broken clay pots like us? How does it happen that God should let our prayers be answered in such intimate and undeniable ways? It's as though He is tapping us on the shoulder and saying, "Do you recognize Me?" It was the first of hundreds of times that God allowed me to see His hand so lovingly and intimately touch His children as He drew them home to Himself.

Mary Anne asked if I had a friend, a priest perhaps, who might come to visit her. I told her that I did. Although we had often spoken about God and His place in our lives, we had never spoken specifically about church or religion, so I was both surprised and happy about her question. I asked a wonderful young man, newly ordained, if he would visit her at home. He was so happy to be asked and would often sit up on the king-size bed with her and share what he had come to know about God and His great mercy and love. I don't know who enjoyed their talks more, because they both seemed to love the give-and-take of shared ideas and they both told of their awareness of God's grace in their midst. They spoke often and long into the night, the wounded healer, healing the wounded. *Which was which*? I wondered. It was an enormous gift to watch this relationship unfold for both of them.

God loves each of His children so deeply and wants them to know Him. His desire for them is to find peace and to come home to Him when He calls. It is wonderful to watch the lengths to which He will go to make that happen. He gives us ample time and uses the everyday gifts we have had all our lives to help us find Him. Mary Anne was gifted with great curiosity and determination, which she had used in her successful business life. God enabled her to use those very same gifts in searching for and finding Him. What an awesome and loving God we have at our disposal all the days of our lives.

One day Mary Anne asked me why I thought God had left her here on earth so much longer than her doctors thought was possible. I said I thought that maybe He wanted to give her all the time she needed to find Him. "Have you found Him yet, Mary Anne?" I asked her one night. "Oh yes," she replied with the same confident assurance she had reflected in business all her life, but this time peace and contentment covered her face.

More than two and a half years had passed since Mary Anne first visited with me. It was Christmas Eve, and once again you couldn't miss God's presence and precious love for her as little children gathered in the snowy night outside her bedroom window, singing "Silent Night." They sounded like angels straight from heaven, and Mary Anne was baptized that very evening by the young priest she had come to know and love very much. Once again God was visiting her Himself through the person He had sent to comfort and guide her on her way home to Him. She died peacefully in the early hours of that Christmas morning.

# Grandfather

*"Who is the man standing*
*down by the water?"*

Grandfather and Grandmother called sounding very sad and frightened. Grandfather had been diagnosed with pancreatic cancer that had spread to his liver. We loved them both very much and wanted to do anything in the world that we could to make this time easier for them. Grandfather said he wanted to be with his only son and grandsons during this final time in his and Grandmother's life together. "Could we come and stay with you?" they asked. "Of course," we said, having no idea about how we would handle everything. Even though I had been a nurse for twenty-five years by then, I had never cared for anyone who was dying in our own home. Our introduction to Paul Brenner, who founded hospice in our city, and the wonderful nurse Dottie Dorion, who cared for us all, made this new experience possible.

Grandfather and Grandmother moved into our master bedroom with the peach carpet, the king-size bed, and the recliner in front of the window overlooking the lake. They felt at home there not because it was their home but because home is where the heart resides and not the house in which we live. All the hearts in this home were now one.

Many a night we served spaghetti suppers, fried chicken, and ice cream for the whole family on that peach carpet. Friends would stop by for a sing-along complete with guitars and off-key voices. Others came to pray with Grandfather, hold his hand, or just sit quietly looking out the window while Grandmother got the chance to wash her hair. Grandfather would look out from his bed at the gathering and say, "This is just how it should be." He was at home, safe with family, where he was loved. That is how he had lived his whole life, simply, in an uncomplicated, quiet, and steady way. He didn't talk about his illness or the fact that he was dying. That would have been out of character for him. It was sufficient for him to be safe, well cared for, with family, and unafraid.

One day, Father Seamus O'Flynn, a new priest at our parish, was visiting with Grandfather and Grandmother in the master bedroom. He was talking to them in his usual kind and gentle voice and helping them to understand that the time was drawing near for Grandfather to go on to God. While he was doing so, Grandfather wordlessly took his wedding ring off his finger and placed it gently into Grandmother's hand. This was the beautiful girl he had married forty-four years earlier. She had been his life partner, his loving wife, and in many ways his caregiver through many challenges and illnesses during their lives together. She was the one to whom he turned when days were dark and fearful and who always kept the home fires burning and a pot of good food on the stove. He found comfort and humor in her oft-spoken words "This too shall pass," even when he didn't think it would. He was beginning the process of separating from her now, quietly, wordlessly, the way they had communicated during their lives together. For those who had shared so much, certain things were just understood and needed no words.

One Sunday afternoon, his son, George, was sitting in the bedroom with him. "Please take down these names, phone numbers, and addresses," Grandfather said as he read off all the names of his friends and co-workers at Horn & Hardart, the Automat in New York where he had worked for forty years. "Go and call them," he said. "Tell them how I am and tell them what is happening to me." George left the room with the names and telephone numbers of the most important people in his father's business life and began his calls. Grandfather trusted George with this important task and knew he would do exactly as he was asked. When George returned, Grandfather wanted to know what each person had said about him and if they understood. And he in turn remembered with great humor the good old days and the forty years of working with them. George recounted each and every conversation and assured Grandfather that his former co-workers felt he had played a major role in all their lives and that they loved him very much. It was important for him to know that those he had worked with and cared about all that time cared about him now too. It was an important step for him. He was beginning to say good-bye.

Grandfather was surrounded with lots of love and good humor during the next few weeks. Friends stopped by, often bringing good things to eat, singing hymns, and telling stories. His cousin Joe, who was like a brother to him, reminisced about the backyard parties that had been such a part of all our lives. His niece Sandra, whom he had raised, told him what it meant to her at age fourteen to be able to live with them after her mother died and how much she loved him.

Grandfather did not grow up in the church and came to faith later in life. He lived out his faith as he did so many things, without much fanfare or fuss. His daughter Janet was with him now as well, and the quiet comfort brought to him and to Grandmother was evident every day and in every way by all she did for both of them. Her conversations with him about God and His love for him were called "a crash course in Jesus" by all of us. He would often turn to Grandmother and say, "Do you believe in all of this, Mother? Well, then I do too."

He was declining rapidly by now and loved sitting each day in the recliner by the window overlooking the lake. On the evening before Grandfather died, Father Dan Logan came by for a visit and to see if he could help in any way. We needed him at the very moment he arrived, as Grandfather was telling us that he wanted to get out of the bed, and we could not manage him on our own. Father Logan lifted Grandfather from the bed and into his favorite chair with ease and without hurting him. We often thought later that on some level Grandfather knew that his days on earth were coming to a close, and he simply did not want to die in our bed. It would have been so like him to think that way.

"Who is the man standing by the lake?" he asked, pointing out of the window.

"That's the weeping willow tree," I said to him.

"I see the tree," he answered with a smile. "I mean the man who is standing underneath the tree, by the water. Who is he?"

I looked but saw no one standing near the tree.

That night while putting my youngest son, Ken, to bed, I told him what Grandfather had said.

"Do you think he saw Jesus?" he asked.

"I don't know," I replied.

Later in the evening as we were preparing Grandfather for bed, I relayed my conversation to Grandfather. "Ken wants to know if you saw Jesus under the tree tonight."

"Yes, dear, why?" he replied. He answered in that same sure, confident, and matter-of-fact way that I have come to recognize and accept in people who are about to die. They seem to have spiritual eyes and ears, understanding things that we do not, and they have no fear of sharing them with you.

Grandfather died that night, sitting in the recliner overlooking the lake where he had seen Jesus, with family members taking turns by his side. When he took his last breath, and we realized it was his last, his wife, son, daughter, and

I all found it comforting for some reason to pile into the king-size bed next to his chair and fall asleep. It was three in the morning.

I mention the time of his death only because when we called his nurse, Dottie, at seven in the morning, she said, "George died at three this morning, didn't he?" When we asked how she knew, she relayed her experience of waking up at three and hearing a voice say, "I've come for my servant George." In the early days of caring for dying patients and their families I only smiled at such things, not really believing them. It took me thirty years of caring for dying people to know that those happenings are as real as anything you will ever experience in life.

Grandfather was a private, kind, and orderly man who loved his family very much. Life was simple for him, and as he was dying it was equally so. Nestled in the comfort of his family's love he felt safe. He died with the same simplicity and grace that he had exhibited all his life. God was equally good to him in both life and in death.

# Frank

*"My son is here with me now;
he said it's time to go."*

Frank was only sixty-eight years old and dying of inoperable lung cancer. He had lived a full and productive life and had a long and happy marriage to Jenny. His diagnosis came as a surprise to him and to his family. He looked and felt well and had only recently been diagnosed with very few symptoms. He was sad that he would be leaving his wife so soon, but his nature was very laid-back, and both he and his wife reflected a peaceful acceptance of his illness, which could only be explained by their experiencing death in some other way before. What it was, I did not yet know.

As I was visiting with him just a few weeks after he had been diagnosed, Frank said to me in a very matter-of-fact way, "My son, John, is here with me now; he said it's time for me to go. Can you see him? He's sitting over there in the chair; he is beckoning for me to go with him." By this time I had learned that his only son, John, had died in Vietnam many years ago.

And now Frank, sitting up in his bed, looking not at all like someone who was dying, was seeing him and enjoying his presence. I replied that I could not see him but asked Frank to tell me how he looked. Frank said John looked wonderful in his uniform, young and as handsome as he had always been, and that John was encouraging him to let go and come with him. Frank had had a warm and trusting relationship with this only son, and now he seemed completely unafraid to leave this life as he knew it. It was amazing to see the joy he expressed at the thought of seeing John again. Their faith enabled them to know they would all be together in heaven at a later time. It seems no one ever dies alone; God always sends someone we have loved to accompany us.

In the few short weeks I was with Frank, I was amazed at the peace that surrounded both him and his wife and their acceptance of his illness and imminent death. They enjoyed each day left to them. They adored this only son who had died years earlier, and their faith told them they would see him again in heaven. Frank's wife, though sad at the idea of losing him, thought it wonderful that John had come for his dad.

Frank died several nights after this conversation, in his sleep, without a struggle, at peace with both his life and his death.

# Brian

*"You know I love you so much."*

Brian was the three-year-old only son of a wonderful young couple, and he was dying of leukemia. His parents had done everything, gone everywhere, to stave off the disease that was soon to take his young and beautiful life. They loved this child with such intensity that you could barely separate them, one from another. They sort of morphed together into one gigantic lump of love. Brian was a wise old sage, mature beyond his years with humor, tenacity, and love so reflective of both his parents.

He could test the patience and endurance of a saint, like all three-year-olds can, but the twinkle in his eyes would melt your heart every time. How they held it all together, I will never know.

Brian would often sit in his mother's lap and put his arms around her neck and hold tight. "You know I love you so much," he would say time and again, and she would smile through her tears. She loved him with all her heart and could hardly bear the thought of his leaving her now. She did not believe in an afterlife, or on some days was not sure, so for her, losing Brian was forever. Only later did she have an experience that would comfort her greatly in this regard.

Brian's presence filled any room he entered. His great big smile, impish twinkle, and unyielding determination endeared him to family and friends, nurses and doctors, and anyone who came in contact with him. Brian was a very knowing child. He seemed to have a handle on people and things before the rest of us did and exhibited an understanding far beyond his years and experience.

His preschool class was creating a very special cookbook, like only three-year-olds could, filling it with favorite recipes to share. Brian's contribution read, "Step one: pull the chair over to the phone. Step two: stand all the way up on it. Step three: pick up the phone and dial Domino's." Needless to say, the cookbook was a bestseller, but more importantly it reflected Brian's individuality and the unique gift of his presence to everyone around him.

Brian loved his mom and dad so much and packed a lifetime of love and kisses, laughter and tears into three short years. He loved his dog and cats, Buster, Me Too, and Sweetheart, but they were too big to visit him in the hospital. Brian knew that my Pekinese had just had a puppy, and I promised to bring her by for a visit. One evening I slipped into the hospital with the brand-new puppy in my purse. Brian's eyes were closed when I laid the puppy into his arms and snuggled its face into his neck. He held the puppy tight in one hand

and found a rapidly wagging tail with the other. He smiled a smile that I will never forget, his eyes still closed.

One day after visiting him at home, I sat down at my desk and asked, "Who is this special child?" Without any effort at all, my musing soon became a poem, which I include for you at the end of Brian's story. Over the years, doctors and nurses, social workers, and others who came to know and love Brian and his family have told me that the poem hangs framed above their desks and in their offices. This child was unforgettable to everyone he met.

"Adios, Daddy," he said more often than not when his dad would visit and then have to leave for work. The wording took on a different meaning now. One night while in the hospital, Brian asked his dad to take a newly delivered bouquet of balloons to a little girl across the hall who had just been diagnosed with leukemia. Brian also asked his dad to take down some of his favorite model cars that were taped to the ceiling. Thoughtfully, he chose which cars or toys should be given to other children at the hospital. Eventually, he directed his dad to give away all his cars and trucks, knowing on some special level that he was leaving.

Brian died quietly one evening cradled in his parents' loving arms. Their pain knew no bounds, and it was only their great love for each other that held them so close to each other now. Brian left this world with a better understanding of pure love and joy, but he left it much too early.

On the first anniversary of Brian's death, I sent yellow roses to his mom, who by now was a dearly loved friend.

She called to thank me and to relate a dream that she had the night before. In her dream she was walking in sand up to her tush. As far as the eye could see, there was nothing but sand, and it was hard to walk. Then in the distance she could see a small light, and she started walking toward it. As she got closer, the sand became shallower and shallower until she was finally walking on top of it. Still far away, near the light, she saw what seemed to be a tent made out of canvas (the kind you go camping in). She said that when she got to the tent, she pulled back the canvas flap and peeked inside. "What do you think I saw?" she asked.

"A beautiful lady was holding a little boy, and she was smiling," she said before I had a chance to answer. We spoke of her Jewish heritage and the fact that the tent in the Hebrew Scriptures is reflective of the dwelling place of God. How natural now that God in His infinite goodness would allow her to have the comfort of knowing her child was safe through this experience in her own tradition. She said that nothing that had been said to her, nothing she had read, and nothing that had been explained to her in the past year had given her a greater sense of peace than this dream. "He's safe and loved, I know that now," she said with great certainty.

The pain caused by the sickness and death of a child is impossible to explain or understand, but the gift this particular child was to all who came in contact with him is equally hard to explain. His very short life left an indelible mark and caused all of us who knew him for even this very short time to take a step back and wonder if our lives have enriched the world as much as that of this little one.

### This Child Called Brian

Brian is goodness, gentleness, wisdom and love
Brian is tenderness, funniness, insight and love
Brian is softness, curiosity, independence and love
Brian is searching, forgiveness, Domino's and love
Brian is Me Too, Sweetheart, Buster and love
Brian is nature, wholeness, life and love
Brian is Nancy, Kenny, beauty and love
Brian was born to love, to touch people, warm
      people, teach people
He made a circle and drew us in
Brian is God's reflection to a hurting world

# Gloria

*"I'm going to go now; bye-bye."*

Gloria was eighty-seven and the matriarch of a large African-American family. She lived in a tiny house in a wooded area near a very busy highway. She had raised her family in this beautifully kept wooden structure, which had obviously been loved and tended to carefully. Over many years she had educated her children, all of whom had gone to college. Family life had been filled with strong faith, church attendance, choir practice, and discipline. You could say this was a "faith-filled family."

On my first visit, I could see that Gloria was in charge. She called all the shots, and her family revered her. They knew that she was declining quickly but found it hard to let her go. There seemed to be someone or something missing, something not yet in place according to plan. Her family hovered over her day and night, trying at every turn to anticipate and meet all of her needs. Time passed quietly.

At one point, Gloria had been unresponsive with no intake or output for about three days, and her respirations were barely detectable. Her very large and loving family never left her side. One night I stayed until midnight, believing that each breath would be her last. It was not to be; Gloria had other plans, and she simply was not ready to go. The family sang beautiful hymns to her, recited some of her favorite Bible verses, and praised God for her life. It was amazing to see the joy and sorrow on their faces but also to hear the very carefully nurtured faith they had been taught by her, expressed with such gusto. *Who or what is she waiting for?* I wondered. When asked by her family to pray with her, I did so quietly, hoping I could remember the twenty-third psalm, which they all knew by heart. By now it was midnight, and nothing was changing for Gloria. She seemed so peaceful, resting quietly, and so I left for the night.

The next morning I stopped by to see her about 8:00 a.m. "Wait until you see Mama," her family said as I arrived at the front door. This very same lady, who as of last night had not responded for three days, was sitting up in bed with a huge smile on her face. She was as aware and in charge as I had ever seen her. "You pray real good, honey," she said to me as I entered the room, reflecting the fact that she had been very aware of everything the night before, just not responding.

Suddenly there was great activity and excitement at the front door. "He's here now," she said, beaming as her eldest son, the one for whom she had been waiting, finally arrived. "I'm here now, Mama," said the tall, handsome man as he gently bent down to hug and kiss her. Laying her head back on the pillow and looking up at her oldest son's eyes, she said, "I know you are. I'm going to go now; bye-bye." And she closed her eyes and died.

I was speechless. Gloria waited until the one person who would know how to handle everything arrived. He was the one to take her place now and protect and guide this family; he knew it and she knew it, and that was that. Gloria left the family in "good hands," with everything in order, the way she had done all her life. I had never seen anything quite like that before.

In Gloria's life, family hierarchy, authority, and responsibility were all important. Her family was built on a firm foundation of faith in God. Through the challenges and hardships she faced since her birth at the turn of the century, she rested on Him. She had conducted her affairs and a very successful family life in this way, and she left this world with the confidence that her work had great meaning and would be passed on to others.

Gloria lived the life she was dealt to the fullest with a quiet strength built on faith. She started with nothing and accomplished everything—a real-life success story.

# Joshua

## "You mean I don't have to stay, Peter?"

"I was born in this bed, and I'm going to die in this bed," Joshua said to me on my first visit to see him. Here was a thin, frail, elderly man sitting up against pillows, in a large, antique bed that was obviously a family heirloom, telling us all how it would be. His wife and daughter had preceded him in death, and now, with his only son, Peter, by his side, Joshua was stating an important fact.

Joshua was as close to death as I had ever seen a patient on the first visit. He had lost a great deal of weight in recent weeks, was sleeping more and eating less, and had very little output and a barely palpable pulse. He was in the dying process, but something was not yet finished. I always find it an interesting experience to talk with a patient and family about what needs to happen in order that a loved one might feel free to leave. Listening closely to what the patient has to say will usually tell you what you need to know.

44

I stepped into the kitchen to speak with his son and daughter-in-law. "He is waiting to hear you tell him it's OK to go," I said. "He feels, as your dad, that he is letting you down by leaving you alone, and he will not go until you give him your permission and tell him it's OK." This tall, bright, handsome executive obviously loved his dad dearly and would do anything to help him. Both he and his wife, Cherry, were so open to whatever would bring him peace. We spoke about Peter's mother and sister Kathleen and the strong Christian faith that allowed Joshua to know that they would be waiting for him in heaven.

Often giving permission to go is the most unselfish thing you can do for someone close to death. It is the gift that has no strings and for which there is no return except for the knowledge that you have loved really well until the end. Mutual affection and respect, practiced in life, are in place when you need them at the end. Trust is an all-important factor in a person's ability to let go if loved ones give permission when it is time. This son and his family loved Joshua very much, and there was nothing they would not do to make this time easier for him.

This wonderful son immediately went back into the bedroom and, getting up onto the bed in a straddling position, looked down at his dad in the most tender and intimate way. "Papa, Papa, you can go anytime you feel you're ready," he said. "Mom and Kathleen are waiting for you. I'll be fine, everything is in order."

Rising up on elbows too weak to hold him, with his face close to his son's, Joshua said, "You mean I don't have to stay, Peter?"

"No, Papa, you can leave anytime, I'll be fine," he reassured him.

Joshua lay back on his bed, and looking up at his son, he smiled. He had heard the words he was waiting to hear. Permission from the son he loved dearly to go on to his new life with his family in heaven. He died gently later that afternoon. "It was my finest hour," his son said to me later. "My final gift to my father."

It was as it should be, a gentle, kindly reversal of roles with the child giving permission to his father to leave and to go on to his loved ones in heaven. The comfort this experience brought to both the father and the son was wonderful to see, and for the son it lasted a lifetime.

# Lenora

*"There's an angel who comes
and stands by my bed."*

Lenora was fifty-four years old, the head of a large Arabic family, and dying of a malignant tumor on her brain. Her family never left her side. They loved her and bathed her and fed her, and they did not talk about her dying. She sat up in bed surrounded by pretty linens and pillows and the wonderful smells of freshly cut flowers, and despite the number of people coming and going, there was never any question as to who was in charge. There was a constant flow of good food, friends, and family, and it was clear that this good mother had loved her children well and now they were giving back to her all that she had given to them.

One day while I was visiting, she asked to speak to me alone, and much to everyone's surprise, she excused her entire family from the room. "This big angel comes and stands near my bed," she said to me very sternly. "Right there," she said, pointing to the corner of her bedroom.

"Is he here now?" I asked.

"No, he just comes and goes, and he is always smiling at me. Ms. Nurse, when I see that angel, do you really think I see that angel?"

"Yes, you do," I said. "When you see that angel, he is really here in the room with you." I explained to her that this is a very common experience for people getting ready to go to heaven, and that God often lets people have glimpses of heavenly beings before they get there. She smiled and nodded her head knowingly in agreement. She was right.

Visions of angels, loved ones who have died before us, family members who are far away, sweet smells, beautiful flowers, and angelic choirs are frequent experiences for those who are dying. We can try to explain these things away in lofty, scientific terms, but eventually we come to know that we are not meant to understand everything. In time that is a relief, since we no longer waste time trying to give our understanding and meaning to a dying person's experiences.

Calling her entire family back into the room, Lenora said to them, "When I tell you that I see that angel by my bed, I'm telling you I see that angel." She left no doubt in anyone's mind that day about what she wanted them to understand, and I often think that she knew on some level the comfort this experience would bring to them later on in life.

For those who walk by faith during their lifetime, spiritual experiences at the end of life are readily understood and accepted. A life of devotion to others brings sweet contentment in the end.

Lenora died peacefully a few weeks later surrounded by loving family and friends who could easily be called her earthly angels. They cared for her the way she had cared for them, with constancy and attention. She remained a mother to the end.

# Gene

*"I know where I'm going, and
I'm not afraid to die."*

Gene was only sixty years old when he was diagnosed with cancer of the lung. He had two handsome sons (blond and blue-eyed), one beautiful daughter (black-haired and brown-eyed), and one precious granddaughter, all of whom he adored. Gene had been married for forty-two years to Teresa, who was the light of his life, and together they had raised a good and happy family.

Gene was a born-again Christian and reflected the certainty of one who knows, for sure, to whom he belongs and to whom he is going. Gene prayed openly, arms raised, on my very first visit with him. He dropped to his knees on the floor in front of me when I asked if he wanted me to pray with him. Here was this faith-filled, born-again, terminally ill, Baptist patient praying, as one, with his Irish Catholic nurse; you could almost see God smiling. Gene had a wonderful personality, so full of life, and had a very trusting relationship with the Jesus he knew so well. He loved to talk about Him and how he came to know Him. In many ways, Gene reflected what I call "old wisdom" or "wisdom of the ages."

I was not at all surprised when he told me one day that his great-great-grandfather had been married to a beautiful Native American princess. This explained his daughter's and granddaughter's beautiful, dark-skinned coloring, and although he didn't speak about it often, you knew that he was intrigued and proud of his ancestry. In my mind it explained his openness to spiritual things, and it gave him insights often lost on the rest of us.

Gene began to decline quickly, and as he was doing so, he seemed to be looking for a loved one whose soul he had often spoken about but was afraid was lost. He would call out for her by name, over and over again, but seemed unable to find her. He was anxious and restless in his search for her, so worried about never seeing her again because he feared she was not "saved." You could see him literally trying to find her, and his fear and pain were difficult for his family to watch. There was no way he could ever find rest until he could rely on the compassionate heart of Jesus to comfort him. I reminded him one day during my visit that he had often talked to his loved one about Jesus and His love, and that while we could not know that person's heart, we could trust that God was a merciful and compassionate God who did not want anyone to perish. Often at the end of a person's life, He brings those conversations to mind, using them to draw that person into

His care. Gene became immediately calm, quietly nodding his head in agreement, and he never looked for her again. It is in times like these that hospice nurses depend entirely on the inspiration of the Holy Spirit to comfort those God sends to their care and not on their own limited insights and understanding. It is a gift He gives to be shared with others as He draws them home to Himself.

One night when Gene was very close to his dying time and his whole family was kneeling around his bed, I asked, "Do you want us to pray with you?" Even though Gene had not responded for three to four days and was too weak to do so now, he made it known to everyone with a moan and shake of his head that, yes, he would like us to pray.

As we were praying it became evident that he could hear us, and we found him praying along with us. Slowly but surely he raised himself up to a sitting position, arms held high above his head and praying with words that were near and dear to his heart. Finally, after what felt like a very long time, he eased himself down on the bed and fell into a restful sleep. Gene knew God very well in the person of Jesus Christ. He had a very intimate and trusting relationship with Him and died with the full knowledge that he was loved, forgiven, and saved.

# Elliott

*"Unless a grain of wheat falls to the ground."*

Elliott was a fifty-two-year-old physician, very esteemed by his colleagues and beloved by his family and friends. He was dying of colon, liver, and lung cancer, and he was dying quickly.

The pressures of life had caused Elliott to turn to alcohol early in his career, and it had been very painful for his family. He wanted to talk about that time in his life, how it was for him and how sorry he was to have put his family through so much pain. But even more, he wanted to talk about how God had made His presence known to him during his darkest days. He came to know forgiveness in a whole new way, he said, and since that time he had "talked and walked with Him daily." This new and humbling relationship with Jesus Himself had enabled him to stop drinking completely and allowed him to lead a loving and productive life ever since.

Sometimes people who have been addicted to alcohol and other drugs seem to have a more difficult time dying than do others. Perhaps the fears that had been with them all their lives and caused them to depend on alcohol manifest themselves even more vigorously when their bodies are frail and less able to fight the fears off.

Elliott confided to me one day that on more than one occasion "a creature" came into his bedroom during the night and frightened him. He said that it leaned up against him in the bed and was very ugly. He explained it to me in minute detail and felt it was an "evil essence," perhaps one of the old and unknown fears he had referred to in the past. He didn't quite know what to do about it. We spoke about the fact that evil is real and that when we are tired or sick or vulnerable, we cannot allow ourselves to be overcome by it. Elliott decided that prayer was what he needed most at these times and promised to pray if the experience repeated itself. It did, just a few nights later, and this time Elliott was ready. Since he had come to know Jesus years before and was very comfortable speaking to Him personally, he simply demanded that the "creature" leave him in Jesus's holy name. He needed to do this only once, and when he did, the creature never came back.

Who is this God whom people like Elliott speak about so often? How is it that He makes Himself known in such vivid and tender ways when we need Him most? Does He really know how it will be for us when it is our time to go home to Him? Does He want to create a soft pillow of insight and understanding on which we can lay our heads? Does He really walk that closely with us all our lives so we can go to Him in the end feeling safe and free from fear? Elliott thought so, and it was wonderful to watch the intimacy with which it was done.

Elliott felt strongly that all of life had purpose and meaning, the good as well as the bad. He said often that during life we are called to learn the lessons sent to us by God. He loved having me tell him about the story in one of my favorite novels, where St. Paul is walking on the hill at Calvary and stands looking at the three crosses there. As he is watching, the center cross on which Jesus hangs falls backward into the ground. "What do you see in the fields behind the cross?" I would ask him. "Wheat fields. That's what it's all about," he would say with obvious insight and understanding. "Unless the grain of wheat falls to the ground during our lives, it cannot bear fruit for our eternity." In his mind, Elliott felt that in his dying to self and alcoholism and in depending totally on the mercy and goodness of God, he was able to be truly free to live for the first time in his life.

Elliott died peacefully one evening with his loving family beside him. He was unafraid and at peace with both his life and his death and the lessons God had taught him along the way.

# Steven

*"I want to have everything in
order; will you help me?"*

Steven was not yet fifty. He was married for the second time
with a daughter who did not know she was adopted, older
children, and a ten-year-old son for whom life held many
challenges.

Diagnosed with cancer of the stomach and fatigued by the
many inconveniences and discomforts of his disease, Steven
seemed to be declining quickly and trying hard to get everything in order. His physician felt that Steven was not dying
anytime soon and that many of his symptoms were brought
on by medication. He thought it must be the morphine that
was making Steven so sleepy and sapping all his energy.

I saw the situation differently. Not because I was smarter
but because of the things Steven was talking about wanting to
accomplish before he died. He was impatient and in a hurry,
and I simply followed his lead. When you are a nurse, you

learn to let the patients tell you in word or in deed what it is they want you to know and to help them with.

He spoke to me at length about his young son, his concern and love for him as he made long-range plans and arrangements for him to be educated at a boarding school after he died. He loved each of his children very much and wanted them all to know that. He wanted to settle everything himself so none of them would be called on to handle things that they should not be responsible for.

"Your patient is dying," I said to his physician one day, "maybe in forty-eight to seventy-two hours."

"How do you know that?" the doctor asked.

"Because he's doing many last-minute things and because he tells me he's dying," I said. His physician was about the same age as Steven and could not fathom that he could be dying so young. He made arrangements for Steven to be seen at a large medical center in another city the next day.

A short and uneventful trip to the medical center did not alter the course of Steven's condition, and although new tests, more blood work, and scans were ordered, everyone but the physician could see that Steven was dying quickly.

A large group of family and friends had traveled to be with him now. One cousin, who was like a brother to him, asked me what they all could do for him that night that would be good for Steven. I asked what they would ordinarily do when getting together. He said that they would gather at each other's houses, dance the polka, and sing wonderful Polish ballads. I encouraged them to stay all night and do just that.

Steven's physician, who still felt that Steven had lots of time, was in full agreement with the plan. The nurse on duty told me the next day that she had never heard such a happy, singing group in her whole life. His cousin and all his friends told the funny stories about each other that wove the fabric of their lives together. They told Steven how much they loved him and thanked him for the good memories that were so clearly etched in all their hearts since childhood.

Steven died early in the morning with all of his best friends giving him the send-off of a lifetime. He had completed all the plans needed for the welfare of his children and his family and had spent his last hours with those who loved him best. It was, as it should be, living life to the fullest to the end.

I called Steven's doctor in the morning to let him know. He was shocked at the gentle and rapid death his patient had experienced but was glad to know that the end was so happy for him. He said that he did not plan on dying anytime soon, but that when it was his time, he sure hoped I'd be around to tell him.

# Robert

*"Pray with me again, honey."*

Robert was only fifty-four years old and dying of lung cancer. He was a happy and loving man who had called all the shots in his life, a real "in charge" kind of guy. He had raised two good sons with discipline and humor and had been married to his beloved Dot for more than thirty years. On my first visit, Robert let me do all the talking, and when I was finished, he simply said, "I'm glad, young lady, that you are my nurse. Now, please tell me, when am I going to die?" He no more looked like he was dying than I did.

I explained to him that his physician and oncologist could tell him all about his medical condition, his blood work, and his prognosis. But when the time was getting closer, God would speak to him in his spirit and He would let him know when his time was near. He seemed content with that answer.

Robert continued to live his life well, sitting outside on the patio in the afternoons and enjoying time with his family and friends. His dry sense of humor remained intact, and he could and would spin the yarn with the best of them. His home continued to be filled with family and friends coming and going, just as it had always been.

Although his condition was worsening and he was becoming fatigued more easily and often, he never really took on the look of someone who was dying. Robert had a type of cancer that often does not have the wasting effects that most cancers do. Some disease processes are such that the person loses very little weight, their color remains good, and they experience little to no change in appetite. These patients leave you questioning what is really happening and wondering if a wrong diagnosis has been made. Such was the case with Robert.

One morning Dot called early. "Robert wants you to come by and see him now," she said. "He asked for you as soon as he woke up." I left for his home immediately and found all his family gathered there. When I entered his room Robert said to me, "Do you remember what you told me the first time you visited me about my dying time? Well, today is my day." He was sitting up in bed, with a big smile on his face, looking as normal as blueberry pie. You could have fooled me!

"Pray with me, honey," he said very naturally to me. So we sat on the floor next to his bed and prayed together. "Thank you," he said, patting my hand. "You can go back downstairs now." Robert was a very private man, so hovering was not the thing to do. His family understood and loved each other very much, and they knew the way each person needed to be loved and cared for. They knew that Robert felt his time was near, and they simply believed him. They spent the day with friends coming in and out as had been their habit and lifestyle, and many a funny story was shared that afternoon.

A few hours later, Robert asked that I come back upstairs. "Pray with me again, honey," he said. And so we did.

Robert's early background was Catholic, but he and Dot had married and raised their children in the Presbyterian church. Somehow or other, those who have been raised in the Catholic church yearn for the familiarity of its rituals and sacraments at the end of their lives. They find great comfort in hearing and saying once again with friends and family the prayers with which they were so familiar in their youth. "That's right, honey," he said, patting my hand and smiling. "That's right." It was evident to everyone who knew and loved him that Robert was very much at peace with his life and now with his impending death. He died later that evening in his own room and in his own bed, cared for with love and respect by his family and friends and in charge until the end.

Robert had been a practical man, a realist who saw things as they were and not the way he wished they could be. He was the quiet type, the one who plugged away with one foot in front of the other and no looking back. A good, solid man, a loving husband who was now leaving his responsibilities to his sons, who he knew would handle them well. No reason to linger—just do what has to be done, and do it well.

# Jack

*"I can see the tapestry of my life."*

I was asked to stop by on a Friday afternoon to admit a forty-seven-year-old man into our hospice program on my way to a weekend retreat in St. Augustine. Jack was dying quickly of very advanced lung cancer and was anxious to talk. During my three-hour stay, Jack asked a "zillion" questions about his disease, how I thought he would do, what would happen to him, and what it was like to die. He wrote down our conversation, both the questions he was asking and the answers he was looking for, on the pad he held in his lap. He told me about the "tapestry of his life" that God had been showing him and explained carefully what the different colored threads meant and where they had taken him. He said he understood now the choices he had been given and the options he had chosen, and like so many other patients I cared for, both before and after

Jack, he seemed not at all saddened by what he saw, only enlightened and comforted.

I left for my weekend retreat, which was conducted by an old Franciscan priest who told us right off the bat that he had not been scheduled for this weekend, but that the priest who was had gotten "the gout." His topic for the weekend was "The Tapestry of Our Lives," the very topic Jack had spoken with me about. During the weekend, the old priest answered each and every question Jack had brought up to me, and I could hardly write fast enough to take it all down. This was no coincidence, and his words were just too important and too personal not to share with Jack.

When the retreat ended on Sunday, I received a phone call from Jack's wife, Sarah, and his family saying that he would like me to stop by again that evening to talk. His parents were with him now, visiting from out of town, and wanted to know whether or not they should leave to go back home. Seeing a significant change and decline in Jack in only two days, I suggested they plan to spend the night, which they did. This was their only son.

Stepping into Jack's room, I pulled out all of my notes from the retreat as he looked over his pad of questions. We reflected on his "tapestry of life" understandings and reviewed together, one after another, all that the old priest had to say. Each and every pondering on his pad was answered in the most awesome and intimate way by the priest's explanation. It was unbelievable to both Jack and his wife to hear the answers God was giving to him.

Jack was a very pragmatic man—thinking things through, reviewing the past carefully, and asking questions and finding answers for the future. God knew him well and allowed him to have the important questions answered in the most unlikely way and by a most unlikely person. Who could ever have guessed that the questions Jack would ask on that first visit would be answered in their totality three days later by an old priest who was not scheduled to conduct the retreat at all. Ours is an awesome and faithful God.

Over the last three days, Jack had been doing lots of thinking, and in that time God had been revealing Himself to him even more intimately than before. It seems that Jack's daughter had been living with her boyfriend, and Jack had been debating about whether or not he should tell her how he felt about that. He did not want to alienate her from him, but as God the Father was revealing Himself to Jack and gently letting him know the truth about life, Jack knew he should be doing the same for his daughter. As we were speaking about this, a knock came to the door and his young daughter walked in. She curled up on the bed beside him as I excused myself from the room. Just a few short minutes later his daughter came into the living room beaming, and a quick look in on Jack brought a broad smile and nod of his head. Work accomplished. The timing could not have been more perfect.

Jack's lung cancer was such that his physician had confided to me that Jack would have a very difficult death. His lungs would fill with fluid suddenly, he would be unable to breathe with comfort or ease, and he would have to be heavily sedated at the end to give him any relief at all. He suggested that we stay in close touch and agreed to order whatever was needed for Jack to have a peaceful death.

"If I am a Christian," Jack asked when we were finally alone, "and know where I am going and believe in God, then why am I afraid to die?"

We spoke together of Jesus's life and death, with which he was very familiar. We spoke about the night before He died and how in the Garden of Gethsemane, He asked His disciples to stay awake with Him because He was dreading what He knew was ahead of Him, and He did not want to be alone.

I explained to Jack that if Jesus, the Son of God, was afraid and wanted the company of friends as He was about to die, then why should Jack think he was any different. Although Jesus is God, we as Christians believe He is also man, and it was that part of Him that recoiled at the prospect of what lay ahead of Him. Jack liked the thought of being both afraid and accepting of God's will and found great comfort in his experience being likened to what Jesus Himself experienced.

"When you wake up in the middle of the night and feel afraid," I told him, "ask Sarah to come and hold your hand and stay with you until you go back to sleep."

At three in the morning, Jack woke up and called Sarah to come and sit with him and hold him so he would not feel alone. She did just that. He died in her arms within minutes, without a struggle, peacefully and with no medication to sedate him. His doctor could not understand how Jack's death could happen so easily. I shared with him our conversation of the night before about Jesus's death and explained how both his new insights as well as his wife's presence allowed him to die gently, in safety and peace.

# Mark

*"There it is. I can see it. It's beautiful."*

Mark was a handsome forty-seven-year-old man who had been diagnosed with pancreatic cancer that had spread to his stomach and liver in a very short time. He had been an outgoing and athletic man all his life, and he and his wife enjoyed a full and happy life together. This new and very deadly diagnosis came as a great shock to both of them as all their plans came to an abrupt stop. He was six foot five and in a very short time down to 125 pounds and dying quickly, and both he and his wife knew it.

They lived in a beautiful condominium overlooking a golf course with lily ponds and palm trees everywhere. Although Mark knew he was dying, his physician, with whom he had a wonderful and trusting relationship, was torn as to whether or not he should do additional exploratory surgery to make sure Mark did not have an abscess in his abdomen. Mark was so young, and after all, he thought, wasn't there something he could do for him? In a late-night conversation with his physician, I asked if it might be possible for him to visit Mark and his wife at home. Upon discovering that they lived very near his office, he agreed.

That evening after office hours, he stopped by and spent time with Mark and his wife. He called me immediately after to say it was the most important thing he had been able to do for Mark and he was so glad he went. He saw him in beautiful surroundings with loved ones and friends, pain free and ready to die. For Mark, the visit held great meaning as well because he and his doctor had become friends, and this would be their last meeting together. It was time to say thank you and good-bye.

I explained to the young home health nurse who would be spending the night with him that Mark was very close to his dying time and suggested that she should not be surprised at anything she might see. She confessed that she had never been with a dying patient before and was a little apprehensive. I reassured her as best I could, giving her my home phone number and encouraging her to call at any hour, about anything. I did not expect Mark to live through the night.

The call came at 4:00 a.m. Mark had died. Would I come? Mark's wife and the nurse explained excitedly that Mark's breathing had changed very quickly. Suddenly his eyes opened wide, and, sitting up in bed under his own strength with arms raised in the air and a big smile, he said, "There it is. I can see it. It's beautiful." And lying back down he took his last breath and died.

His wife felt that Mark had seen a glimpse of heaven just as he entered, and she was both awestruck and comforted by the thought that he was excited by what he saw there.

Mark loved both his wife and his life very much and did not want to leave either one. But he had lived and loved really well in those forty-seven years, more so than many people do in a long lifetime. Surrounded at the end by those who knew and loved him best and feeling very safe in his surroundings, he was able to die with the dignity and grace he had exhibited during his life. The fact that his physician remained close to him and genuinely cared about him gave him great comfort as well. This is what is often referred to as a "good death."

# Marian

*"I have never known my mother
to have such peace and calm."*

Marian was young, in her fifties, living alone and dying of ovarian cancer. She lived in a small, cluttered trailer near a busy road and was resting in a hospital bed in the corner of the tiny bedroom the first time I visited with her. Her young son, home on medical leave from the army, was caring for her with great love and tenderness. I could immediately see that Marian was actively in the dying process, suffering a great deal of both physical and emotional pain. She never opened her eyes during the thirty minutes I visited with her, and her hands were white knuckled as they held on to the bed rails on either side of the bed. I asked her son if she had a minister or priest that she might like to have visit her, and he said no. "She was raised Catholic," he said, "but she married many times. She doesn't want any priest or preacher now, only the last rites just before she dies." But it seemed God wanted more for her.

I sat alone with Marian in the tiny corner of the trailer that was her bedroom and explained that God was making a place in heaven for her. I told her that He loved her very much and only wanted her to come home to Him and to feel safe in His arms. I told her the story of the Good Shepherd and how He loved all the sheep in His fold equally, even the ones who had wandered away for a time. I reminded her that we all wander during our lifetimes and lose our way, but that God goes out of His way every time to bring us back. We are all that one sheep that He never loses sight of, and I have often seen just how long and how far He will go to help us find our way back to Him.

I told Marian that I had a wonderful friend who was a Catholic priest, and that I knew he would come to see her if she wanted him to. I tried in every way I knew how to comfort her and assure her of God's great acceptance of and love for her. She gave no hint at all that she heard anything I said, keeping her eyes tightly closed and a firm grip on the side rails of her hospital bed.

Having obtained pain medication for her and instructing her son on how to give it, I left, assuring him I would call back shortly to check on her and telling him he could reach me for anything by calling my beeper.

Two hours later while at a funeral service for another patient, I received a call from Marian's son. "Did you tell my mother you have a friend who is a Catholic priest who would come to visit her?" he asked. "Well, she wants him to come to see her now."

Following the funeral, I told Father Seamus O'Flynn of my need for him to see Marian right away. He canceled a luncheon appointment and went directly to her. Three hours later her son called to say that in all the years he had known his mother, he had never known her to have such peace and calm. "She looks so beautiful," he said, "just so beautiful, and she is smiling." God wanted Marian to know how much He loved her, and He sent this gentle priest to assure her of that love. It was a great gift for her, but an even greater gift for her son, who saw the healing touch of God's mercy for the first time in his life. Marian's son and I stayed in touch for many years, and he often spoke about the priest's visit that special afternoon and the effect it had on his mother's last day. Equally as important, he said, it had changed his life as well.

Marian died peacefully that evening with her son holding her hand, with the full knowledge that God loved her and that she was assured of her place in heaven, safe and unafraid.

# Lennie

*"Will you let me know when
it's my time to go?"*

Lennie was in his mid-fifties, diagnosed with cancer of the
colon with widespread metastatic disease to the bone. He
and his wife were poor, living off the land out in the country
on meager earnings, with three small sons. His family loved
him dearly, looking out for him with tender loving care, and
they were the only concern in his life.

"Help me to live as long as I can and to do as much as I can
between now and when I die," he said to me. "And when it is
my time, will you let me know?" I assured him that I would
do everything he asked me to do for him and his family and
that I would let him know when it was his time.

Lennie's condition declined rapidly. He ate less and slept
more hours each day, and his pain was finally well controlled,
which was very important to him and his family. He was alert
and as busy as his illness allowed him to be, with each day

having some happiness and meaning in it. He spent time with each of his sons, talking and loving them for hours on end, planning with his wife for the time when he would no longer be with them.

Lennie had shared with me the one major concern he had for his young sons. "I don't want the last picture my boys have of me to be on a stretcher, dead and being taken out the front door," he said. "If you'll tell me on the day you think I will die and arrange for me to go into the hospital and be comfortable, I'll be very grateful." I promised him that I would.

One morning, I visited Lennie at home and realized he was actively in the dying process. "It's time to go to the hospital now," I said to him, and he smiled a gentle and accepting smile in agreement. He told his sons he needed to go to the hospital for a while, and they could see him there later in the day. They did not understand that Daddy would not be coming home again, but the bravery on that dad's face and the utterly selfless act of thinking only of his sons is forever etched in my soul. There was no time to waste.

Following some hasty footwork, we were able to have him admitted to the local hospital with little time to spare. Sitting up in bed, weak but smiling, he asked to see his sons, one at a time, and then his wife. One by one the little ones entered his room alone, closing the door behind them. He told each of them that he would be going away, on to the heaven they all believed in, and explained what he expected of each of them. Talking about their future as if he would continue to be part of it, he assured them that he would be watching over them and knew they would grow into young men he would always be proud of. It was heart stopping to see their little faces and hear these important words spoken so bravely by this father.

When all the visits were finished, Lennie asked to be alone with his wife. The children sat quietly just outside his door. My last view of them was together, curled up in the bed holding each other. He died in her arms one hour later.

Lennie was a father in the truest sense of the word. He was actively involved in his sons' lives every day, and it seemed only natural that he felt he would always remain that way. He knew each of them well and spoke to them in a way that reflected that at the end. What he did and how he did it showed the intimacy of his relationships, and I have no doubt at all that they remember to this day what he said to each of them.

# Jackson

*"Do you know how much God loves you?"*

Jackson was sixty-four years old and looked every bit of ninety. An old sailor, toothless and unkempt, he had been, according to his own account, on the fast track of "wild women and song" for most of his youth and adult life. Now as he was dying, he asked to come back home to one of his former wives to be cared for by her at the end. I often had conversations with God after one of my visits to Jackson, asking Him to never put me in a situation like the one He put Jackson's ex-wife in. I wasn't at all sure that I would be kind enough to handle it so well.

On the very first day I visited with him, Jackson confessed all of his sins to me in minute detail, much of which I could have lived a lifetime without hearing. He did so with all the humility and honesty you could imagine. He seemed to want to tell someone everything about his life and all the things he had done and all the wrongs he had committed. His face and words revealed such sorrow and remorse, and my heart went out to him. "Have you any idea how much God really loves you?" I asked him when he was finished. "Do you know He forgives you all your sins because you are sorry for them and you have told Him so?"

Throwing both frail and withered arms into the air, he said loudly, "Yes, I do!" I was amazed and taken aback by both the certainty and force with which he spoke. Was this what Jesus meant when He spoke of the man in Scripture with greater faith than He had seen in all of Israel? I think I was seeing and hearing this faith right then and there with this very repentant soul.

Jackson knew what forgiveness meant from God's perspective. Somehow, he knew that you don't earn your way into heaven, but you get there because Jesus died for you, because He loves you. I think he knew that forgiveness begins the moment we recognize the wrongfulness of our actions and are sorry for them.

Jackson died peacefully one night, alone, but safe in his Father's arms, trusting totally in His love and forgiveness.

Jackson did not think he had gotten off easy or that God was just a soft touch who would overlook everything. He had been a great sinner in his own eyes, but somehow he knew that God's love was bigger than his sins. His humility allowed him to accept forgiveness, to repent, and to die peacefully. The lessons you learn from those you serve are important ones, and they stay with you for a lifetime. It seems the bigger the sin, the gentler the hand of God.

# Hank

*"You didn't tell me, did you? How did you keep it a secret?"*

Hank was in his early seventies, living with his wife of forty-some years and dying of lung cancer. Their only child was in prison for a heinous murder, and no request on our part, through correspondence, in person, or otherwise with congressmen, chaplains, wardens, or local officials could change the fact that Hank would never see Shawn in person again.

Each time I visited, Hank would say, "I'm not going to die until I have seen Shawn, you know. I have things I need to tell him and things I need to ask him to do."

I prayed so hard that somehow, something could be done. I asked God to intervene for this father and son and give Hank peace before he died. I begged Him for a miracle that would allow them to see each other, but I didn't know what that would be since all avenues had been exhausted as far as I could see.

One Thursday, late in the afternoon, I stopped by to visit Hank and his wife. Hank, who was dying by now, was resting in bed with a beautiful, broad smile on his face. "You didn't tell me," he said with a twinkle in his eye as I entered his room. "How did you keep it a secret?" Thinking quickly and smiling back at him I said, "No, I sure didn't tell you, did I?" Patting the edge of the bed, he indicated that he wanted me to sit down and listen.

"Shawn came by to visit me today," he said. "He stayed about an hour. He looked wonderful." He pointed to the side of his bed where Shawn had sat, and explained in minute detail everything Shawn had been wearing, what color it was, and how he looked. Hank's main concern for his son was that he know that Hank loved him very much and had forgiven him. Equally as important, Hank wanted to ask him to stay in touch with his mother, to call her and love her, even though he would spend the rest of his life in prison. Shawn agreed and promised his father that he would take care of her in the best way he could. All of this seemed very natural to Hank, and he explained it in very simple terms. Being able to see his son, reviewing his visit with him, and hearing his son's promise to him about his mother were very comforting to Hank. I have seen the certainty and naturalness that accompanies these unexplained experiences so many times over the years, and I have to admit, it always takes my breath away. His wife, on the other hand, could hardly believe that Hank truly believed he had seen Shawn and could recount the event so clearly and in such detail.

The pastor from Hank's Methodist church, who was visiting later that afternoon, explained to us that since God is God, He can do anything, and he reminded us that Jesus, following His death and resurrection, had entered the upper room to be with His apostles without opening any door. Why did we question His ability to allow Hank to experience whatever and whoever He knew would give him the peace to let go and come home to Him? Hank died the next evening a happy and grateful man.

# Merideth

*"I can't die until I see Walter."*

Merideth was only fifty-four years old and was dying quickly of cervical cancer that had spread throughout her body. She had raised four children alone, after divorcing her husband of twenty years for having an affair with her best friend and neighbor.

Merideth should have died by now, her oncologist said. "She is down to skin and bones and just won't let go. You need to find out why and what is holding her." She was blessed to have a physician who was in tune with not only her body but with her mind and her spirit as well. He knew it was her time, and he wanted her to be able to let go in peace.

There was very little time to discover what was keeping Merideth on this earth, but following a short discussion with her children, I started to understand. Merideth had long ago forgiven her husband for the pain he had caused her and their children in leaving them, but she had never told him so in person. She understood him so well and knew that without her forgiveness he would never be able to forgive himself. Her concern was that after her death, he would always feel guilty and never be able to find peace and be the father her children would need. "No," she said, "I can't die until I see Walter. I just can't."

We needed to make this happen right away.

Many phone calls later, I finally reached Walter one afternoon at about five o'clock. I explained Merideth's circumstances and condition and the fact that she needed to see him right away. He was on the next plane and in her bedroom later that same evening.

Merideth and Walter stayed alone in her bedroom for hours. He told us later that she shared with him the fact that she had forgiven him completely a long time ago and that she wanted him to hear that from her now. She wanted him to forgive himself as well before she died. She said she knew that was a hard thing to do, but if he could, he would be a better father to their grown children, because the slate would be clean. She wanted them to know and love each other, and this was the only way she knew to make that happen.

She could have chosen to hold her husband in unforgiveness all those years, but she did not, and in so doing she freed herself as well. Now as she was dying, she wanted to be equally sure that Walter would be free to love his children and be loved by them in return.

In the quiet setting of that bedroom, they each forgave the other and themselves for all that had transpired between them. They gave each other that final gift of peace, allowing Merideth to die quietly during the night, while her children and Walter stayed by her bedside.

# Ralph

*"My wife always wanted me to go to church
with her, but I didn't. Just stubborn, I guess."*

Ralph was a crusty seventy-four-year-old man with cancer
of both lungs, which had also spread to his spine. His wife
and two sons loved him a great deal, but he was unable to
show much affection toward them. He was always there to
meet their everyday needs of food, shelter, and clothing, but
he was unable to show the normal amount of affection one
would expect to see in a family.

There was loneliness in that household that you could
sense at every turn and in every room—an unspoken sadness and the feeling that the people living there had never
really been close to each other but had simply lived under
the same roof. And now they were all trying as hard as they
could to find some kind of common ground between them
so this period of time could be good.

"Are you religious?" Ralph asked me one day as I was visiting him at home (we had become comfortable friends by then).

"Well," I said, "if you mean like always rushing for the first pew in church on Sunday and looking like a goody two-shoes, I hope not. But if you mean, do I love God and believe in Him and believe that He knows me and loves me, yes."

He seemed to like the sound of that. "Well, my wife always wanted me to go to church with her and do church things," he said, "but I never went along with it. I just liked to be stubborn, I guess, never wanted to give in to her and let her think she had her way." Ralph was doing a good bit of reviewing of his life by now, the things he had done well and not done well, what his options had been and how he had handled both the people in his life and their everyday needs. He did not really like what he saw, and he was very honest about it. What would be the answer for him now?

We spent many hours talking about who God was, why He had created us, why He loved us, and where we go after we die. This man, who had never shared much of himself, was now searching for answers and ways to understand his lifetime behavior without really knowing the questions to ask. He, like many of us, had not understood unconditional love and could not begin to understand that God loved him in that way now, warts and all.

He could relate to a "creator," a person in charge, handling things, keeping it all together as he had done. However, as hard as he tried, he found it difficult to understand a God who loved him personally and without reserve. He said he had never experienced that kind of love in his own life when he was young, and consequently he was not able to give or receive that kind of love in his own family. It made for a great deal of sadness, aloneness, and misunderstanding with his sons and wife, and it weighed heavily on his heart at this time in his life.

We talked about Jesus and how God the Father had sent Him, His only Son, to earth to teach us the way to Him. It was a whole new concept for Ralph, but one he was able to take in over a period of time and make his own. I think that at this stage he was so ready to be loved, really loved, that he raced toward this new understanding with arms wide open. It is the empty space inside all of us that St. Augustine speaks about when he says, "Our hearts are made for you alone, Oh God, and they can not rest until they rest in You."

When shopping one day, I found a lovely plaque picturing Jesus walking through clouds with arms outstretched, welcoming someone into heaven. I bought it for Ralph, and he asked me to put it on the wall next to his bed so that he could see it when he turned his head. Looking at it seemed to give him great comfort. As time went on and he began to take in the real meaning of love and life, he and his family were able to spend more quiet time together. He especially enjoyed having his grandchildren around him. Words, which had been foreign between them, essentially remained that way, but Ralph reflected a new measure of peace they had not seen before. He died quietly one evening, with his family in the next room, the way he had lived. Just as in life, he remained somewhat removed from them, but in truth he was always there for them.

Ralph really loved his family very much, but he had no well of memories or experience into which he could dip for guidance. It takes an enormous amount of love and forgiveness all the way around when the circumstances of life present themselves in this way. God remained close to Ralph to the end, enabling him to have a glimpse of unconditional love for the first time in his life. This allowed his family to see a side of him they had never known before, freeing them from the hardness of heart they could have carried the rest of their lives. The lessons to be learned are always on both sides of the coin.

# Carl

*"Soon you will be with Jesus in heaven."*

Carl was seventy-seven years old and living with his third wife in a tiny house set on cinder blocks near the outskirts of town. He was dying of liver and stomach cancer, but you could tell from the start that he was on a mission. It was Thanksgiving time, and Carl seemed to love this time of year, remaining open to all of life until the very end.

Carl was a deeply spiritual man; however, he had abandoned his faith years ago and had not attended church for many years. He did continue to recite the small, familiar prayers he'd said as a child. He was looking for a way back but never seemed to find it. Now, he was searching for a safe way to go home, a way to find solace and comfort from the God he knew had never left him. How would it all come to pass? In what way was God going to draw Carl back to that peace and safety he was longing to find?

December came, and the Living Nativity, a pageant held each year at my own church, was being prepared. "Would you like to come to see it?" I asked Carl one afternoon during our visit just days before the event was to begin. "We'll see," he said. "We'll see." He needed time to think about it and how much effort it would take to get him there.

"Can you come and get me now?" he asked on the very evening of the event and about an hour before it was to begin. I rushed to his house, and his wife and I bundled him up in his pajamas, bathrobe, and wool cap, and covering him with king-size blankets we drove him to the church, where it had started to snow lightly. Taking his frail body out of the car, we placed him gently in front of the outdoor nativity scene, where church friends had prepared him a special place of honor. Slowly the dim lights came on, snow continued to fall, and the music began to play. Carl was looking directly into the faces of those taking the place of Mary, Joseph, and baby Jesus in the pageant. It was as though they were look-ing directly at him, and he was leaning forward as far as he could so as not to miss any of it. He saw the shepherds, the three wise men, and all the little children dressed as angels. Carl sat motionless with tears streaming down his face as the choir sang "Silent Night" and "O Little Town of Bethlehem." He was never the same man again.

A wonderful peace came over Carl, and he faced each day with a new calm and serenity. Very late one night, he called to ask if I could arrange for him to see a priest. He wondered if the priest could come "right now." Without hesitation and in the middle of the night, my good friend Father O'Flynn went to pay an important visit. He never needed explanations. I only needed to ask and to give him directions, and he would find his way there.

At 3:00 a.m., with his family sitting quietly in the next room, Carl spoke to Father about his life, what he had done well, and where he had gone wrong. When they were finished, Father invited all of his family back into the room. Putting his arms around and under Carl to help me lift him up in the bed, he said to him, "Carl, soon you will be with Jesus in heaven. I know I will see you there someday."

It was a Rembrandt moment! No one could move, no one could breathe. It was a time of comfort and healing for everyone. A Jesus encounter if I had ever seen one.

Carl died that night, looking like he was in heaven hours before he took his last breath.

Carl's prayers all those years were not lost but heard by the God who loved and created him. Who could have dreamed up the Living Nativity scene, with snowflakes in Florida on that cold December night, when God chose to touch Carl's heart and bring him comfort? How do you explain the tender effect this humble priest's words would have on all those present at that early morning encounter? Who but God Himself can think of that many ways to touch His children?

# Louis

*"He doesn't look like Daddy anymore."*

Louis was only forty-one years old, but he was dying. He was the son of Robert, who had been my patient more than eighteen years before and about whom I wrote in an earlier chapter. He was divorced, raising his thirteen-year-old daughter on his own, and dying of the same oat cell carcinoma of the lung as his dad.

Louis had many concerns. Where would he live when he was dying? What would happen to his daughter after his death, and how would he handle things between now and then?

His family insisted he make his home with them. His mother and brother and his much-loved daughter would all be together. Arrangements were made for her to be adopted by her uncle, who had loved her since she was a very little girl. It was settled now, and things would be as good as they could be for a while.

Louis was declining very quickly, but no one at home knew quite how to talk to his young daughter about what was happening. She knew very clearly that her dad was dying and was able to speak at length with her school counselor about how she was feeling, but it was so hard for her to find the words to express herself at home. After much encouragement by all those who loved her best and were around her the most, she finally agreed it was time for her to share her fears and thoughts with her uncle, grandmother, and those involved in her father's care.

"He doesn't look like Daddy anymore," she said tearfully one day. "He can't do anything that he used to. It's so sad." She was used to a strong, young father able to do everything, and it was so hard for her to see him this way. The change was so dramatic and swift that it left a thirteen-year-old very little time to understand any of it and very few words to describe how it felt. When she finally was able to talk, she spoke from the heart about how much she loved him, how much she would miss him, and that she knew she would see him again one day in heaven. It seemed enough for her because the pain of seeing him like this was just too much to bear.

Early one morning Louis's brother called. "Something's different," he said. "Will you stop by?" When I got to the house, Louis was sitting in the den in his favorite chair, talking to his daughter as she was getting ready to leave for school. She came close to his chair, and bending down she hugged and kissed him. He in return looked at her with such loving eyes, knowing full well it would be for the last time.

His eyes followed her to the door as she turned and waved good-bye.

His mother went upstairs to take a shower and his brother left for the store to pick up medications, so Louis and I sat talking together.

He spoke about his disease, what it had done to him, how strange that it was just like his dad's, how fast it all seemed to be happening, and how grateful he was to his mother and brother for loving him and taking care of him and his daughter. We spoke about the fact that his dad would be waiting for him, and he smiled when he suggested that his dad might have a long lecture waiting for him.

After talking for a short while Louis said, "Please walk me toward the door." And standing up quickly he went directly to the front door. "No, no, not that door," he said, walking directly back to his chair. "Take me into the bathroom," he said suddenly, moving so quickly down the hall that I had difficulty keeping up with him. Passing a nearby bedroom, I grabbed a king-size pillow, placing it at his back just as he sat down on the commode. Louis was fading fast, and I prayed hard that his mother would finish her shower and come quickly to him, which she did. When she stepped into the bathroom, she knew immediately what was happening, and standing between the sink and the commode, she wrapped her arms around his shoulders and held him close to her. Just then, the front door opened, and his brother, back from the store, entered the bathroom and knelt down beside him. We all knew Louis was moments away from death.

"God's making your place in heaven now," we said to him. "You'll see a glimpse of it just before you go in." We slipped the pillow from his back to his knees just as he started to lean forward, and resting his head on it he looked his brother straight in the eye and said, "I can already see a little bit of it." And closing his eyes, he died.

We stood there together and smiled, knowing his dad, who had great humor, would be there to greet him, saying, "Couldn't you have come in a more dignified way than on the commode?" We laughed and cried together, the mother who loved him dearly, the brother who was taking care of everything for him, and the nurse who was privileged to experience this precious moment with all of them.

# Delia

*"You'll come to me when it's my time; I'll depend on you."*

Delia's husband, Ralph, had been my patient many years be-fore. We had become good friends in the ensuing years, and each and every time she wrote or called me, she would say, "Remember, now, you'll come to me when it's my time. I'll depend on you." I always reassured her either in person or on the phone, over a great cup of coffee or lunch, that I would be there for her when it was her time.

Delia was getting older now and unable to stay in her own home alone. She had a mind of her own, and it took some convincing by her sons to help her see that she would be much happier if she did not have to worry about keeping up a house anymore. She finally agreed, and her family moved her into a lovely nearby retirement center with wonderful care available, a beautiful view, and the chance to meet new friends. In short order, Delia was contented and asked why her sons had not forced the issue sooner. I reminded her that she was somewhat stubborn and wasn't going anywhere until she was good and ready. She was not settled in for long before a call from one of her sons sent me scurrying to the ICU of one of the local hospitals.

Delia had either suffered a stroke and then fallen down and broken her hip, or she had fallen down first, breaking her hip, and then had a stroke. It was impossible to know which came first, and the time between her fall and finding her was equally hard to measure. Surgery was scheduled for the next day on this elderly, frail eighty-five-year-old in an attempt to try to patch her badly crushed hip. They all knew it was risky surgery, but if she were to have any quality of life she would need to have it done. I think Delia had something else in mind.

When I entered the room that evening, Delia turned her head and looked me straight in the eye with what I have always called "knowing eyes." You could tell by the expression reflected there that she knew everything that was going on around her, everything that was happening to her. Delia knew she was dying, and she smiled as I walked across the room and stood close to her bed, touching her arm gently.

"Do you remember, Delia, that we always said we'd be together when your time came?" I asked. Her eyes filled with tears and she nodded. "Well, this is your time. God is making ready your entrance into heaven, and you'll see Ralph very soon now. Are you ready?" She nodded her head yes, never leaving my gaze for a moment. "Would you like me to pray with you?" I asked. And as she was smiling, she took both my hands into hers, held them next to her heart, and closed her eyes.

I prayed that Jesus would make Himself known to her, that He would put His arms around her and send His Holy Spirit to enlighten and comfort her. I asked her to rest her head on His shoulder and let Him hold her. I could see her turn her head and nestle it into the pillow, like a little child would nestle into its mother's bosom. She was so peaceful.

"So sweet," she murmured. "So sweet." And she dozed off to sleep. Delia had always said that she wanted a friend whom she loved and who loved her to be with her when she entered heaven. What a wonderful gift it was for me to be able to fulfill that promise, made so long ago, to be with her in her dying time. Two hours later Delia entered heaven quietly and would not need that surgery after all.

Who but God Himself could orchestrate an ending like that wherein He answers the prayers of the person He is calling home in such a direct and intimate way? Her sons, who loved her very much, were so relieved she would not need the surgery and that she had found her final peace. They felt she had received the ultimate healing that she longed for all her life. She died the way she wanted to, in the company of a friend.

# Kathleen

*"The kingdom of God is at hand."*

Kathleen was seventy-two years old and lived alone. An elderly sister lived nearby and looked in on her each day, trying as hard as she could to make life better for her. Kathleen had been terminally ill for a long time and had suffered greatly during her illness. Although only seventy-two, she looked every bit of ninety and was so thin and frail she was unable to move about on her own. On my first visit, I could see that Kathleen had a very short time to live, so getting her comfortable and pain free was all-important to her well-being. We arranged for that to happen quickly, and in no time at all she was experiencing good and peaceful days. In the meantime we became fast friends, as so often happens when time is short and words and togetherness are all-important.

When I would get to know my patients, I would often ask them to tell me about their faith. It was enriching to hear how God makes Himself known to people. Kathleen helped me to understand the concept of "the kingdom of God" so often referred to in Scripture and how it relates to the here and now as well as to heaven. She understood the power of prayer and the idea of praying for one another's needs and cares, and how in doing so we experience that kingdom here on earth.

As a mother of four sons, I needed all the help I could get, so I had the habit of asking my patients to pray for my kids. They loved the idea that they had a job to do for me, and many a good chuckle was had when on a bad day with the boys I asked them to speak loudly to the Lord so He would not miss the urgent request.

One day, just as I arrived at her door, Kathleen raised a thin, bony hand upward and smiled the sweetest smile I had ever seen—a heavenly smile, I would say. As she did so she said to me, "Trudy, remember how we have talked about the kingdom of God—well, it is here, at my hand. I do not have to wait much longer." We discovered together that God's kingdom, here on earth, is all around us. We find it in the people He puts on our path and often the path itself that He has us walk. We find it in those who teach us and those from whom we learn. God reaches out to heal our hearts and souls through the experiences He allows us to share together.

Kathleen died a few days later, sure of where she was going and having taught me many new ways of understanding the kingdom of God.

# Robin

*"Love must be like this, and it must be good."*

Robin was thirty-four years old, full of life, its joys, its sorrows, its good and happy times, and all of its voids. Robin was a twin, and he and his sister Melody shared a very loving and special bond. They were like two halves of the same whole, and without words or actions they often knew exactly what the other was thinking, needing, wanting, or expressing.

Robin was dying from a brutal form of malignant melanoma covering most of his body, and all his twin could do was watch, cry, pray, and be his beautiful sister. She tried to be all he needed, and then some. It was, after all, the other half of her that was so sick and dying.

Robin's dad had died one year before. When Robin was diagnosed and it was decided little more could be done for him, he came back to the family's home to be cared for by his ever-attentive, all-giving, and all-loving Italian mother.

There was nothing halfway about Anita. She was strong-willed, faith-filled, and determined with humor and tenacity seldom seen in the world today. She planned to see to it that Robin had the very best of care in her nonstop, full-throttle, leave-no-stone-unturned, no-holds-barred way. My nickname for her quickly became "the Iron Butterfly." She had just lost her husband, and her mother, who was in her late eighties, needed much tender loving care. Now her beloved Robin was dying. How could one mother handle so much sorrow? I learned, in short order, that her entire life was a life of faith and total trust in the love of God and His divine presence around her. She had a resilient spirit that was not easily daunted by anyone or anything.

And there was Robin, right in the middle of things, calling as many of the shots as he could, in great pain but with humor and tenacity and a not-so-little "gotcha" way of getting things done. Since he had never married, we often talked about love, what it was all about, and what it did and did not mean. He was sorting out many things in his young mind, and loving unconditionally was one of them—how else was he to deal with all that was happening to him?

We tried as hard as we could to relieve Robin's suffering as his pain increased. He, on the other hand, was grateful to have the opportunity to offer his suffering to God, spending large amounts of time praying for others. The power this kind of prayer has is immense, and his explanations of how he offered his sufferings to God often left me numb with awe. Where does this kind of faith and love come from?

Father Bob visited him regularly at Robin's mother's request. Did Father Bob know how to minister to Robin, to comfort him, to guide him? I didn't think so. He seemed too formal, not "touchy-feely" enough for my way of thinking. Being Irish and determined, I decided to ask a young, thirty-four-year-old priest from his parish to spend time with Robin. I even visited with the priest one day and discussed how we could possibly make this happen. The priest was the same age as Robin, had similar interests, and could identify with him more closely, or so I thought. He asked that we pray about it and talk again.

One night while I was talking to God about a way to make all this happen and pouring out to Him the way things should go, God made it abundantly clear to me that I should back away. So clear was His message that in the secret recesses of my soul, I envisioned pulling my hands back from a large stove with very hot flames. "Let Father Bob stay exactly where he is," I heard. "I have a work to do in him too."

From that day on, I never questioned God's will for Father Bob to be involved in Robin's life. We spoke often of Robin's plight and the fact that he was dying so young. I shared with him Robin's need to receive permission from a father figure to die, so he could let go when it was time. Father Bob would smile and pat my hand, saying it just wasn't that simple. He was so patient, and we laughed often as we agreed and disagreed, each trying to make the other see their point of view. I think we learned more than we ever realized from each other during those months.

As Robin moved closer to his dying time, the family gathered together even more than before, never leaving him unattended for a moment. They took turns with nightly vigils, with softly lighted candles flickering nearby, and prayers being said night and day. Robin had a special friend, Cheryl, who loved him dearly. It was she who was with him and his family when he died. It seemed so right that someone he loved and who had shared so much time with him and had been so good to him should be with him now.

Days before he died, I was sitting on a step stool next to his bed, holding his hand. Putting his arm slowly around my shoulder, he smiled and said, "Love must be like this, and it must be good." Robin had come full circle in his understanding of unconditional love, which was to him the way God loves us all. It was beautiful to see how clearly he knew it now and how comforted he was by it.

Robin's life was a learning experience, not only for him and those closest to him. It was a school, a journey for each and every person God drew into the circle of his time on earth. We learned so much from Robin himself, from his sister's devotion to him, from his mother's unending love and sacrifice for him, and from all the lessons God presented to us along the unbelievable path of his young life.

One night, when Father Bob was praying alone with Robin, Robin called out to him, "Father, what must I do?" The priest jumped up and stood close to his bed. Taking Robin's hand in his own, he encouraged him to go on to God the Father when he heard Him call for him. He spoke about His plan for him and the ultimate healing he'd find in heaven. Robin so needed this direction from an authority figure. He so needed this man, in this place, at this time to give him the direction and permission he needed to die. God in His infinite wisdom and love put just the right man within Robin's reach, knowing exactly what both Robin and the priest needed most.

After Robin died, I visited with Father Bob and shared my early thoughts and feelings about him, each of us laughing about the other's stubborn ways of thinking. We had a hearty laugh together and spoke about the things each of us had learned. And then he said to me, shaking his head back and forth, "You will never know what God has done for me during this time, never!" Imagine how much could have been lost if God had not made His message abundantly clear to me that day and if I had not listened and obeyed Him. When He wants to get our attention, He will, in one way or another. The lessons we learned through this experience will last a lifetime for both of us.

The loss of Robin to both his mother and sister is impossible to describe. He is as alive to them today as he ever was, and one only has to see them for a moment to remember the enormity of their love and devotion to him. His was a young and meaningful life, very well lived.

# Tim

*"I have my peace now, Trudy."*

Tim was twenty-nine and gorgeous. A great golfer, expert tennis player, and married for the second time to beautiful Rebecca. Between them they shared two adorable daughters and a wonderful new life. Malignant melanoma was the diagnosis, found one year after their wedding on a routine physical with the suggestion to investigate further. Stage four was the word, not good, very little time left. Metastatic disease spread to his liver, stomach, and brain quickly. It all seemed surreal; surely it could not possibly be happening. Tim was just so young, and he loved Rebecca and his girls so much, and they were just starting their new life together. But Tim saw things as they were and not as he wished them to be, and slowly but surely he began putting things in order.

As his disease progressed, Tim was less and less able to do things for himself. Now you can imagine how hard that would be for a man so young and independent and who was accustomed to calling all the shots. Rebecca was ever so sensitive and patient in allowing him to do as much as he could on his own, not wanting to take away any of his dignity. But this was not easy. As his balance became a bigger challenge for him to deal with, I suggested a tripod, which is a three-pronged cane that can make walking easier. At first Tim railed at the thought of something so large and unwieldy and "out there." When he did not want to do something, he did not make a secret of it. But finally and with great reluctance he agreed to try one, on his terms, when no one was looking—and he sheepishly admitted he liked it! Tim was so independent by nature and remained that way until the last day of his life, accomplishing a list of things he had always wanted to do. He was now in a big hurry, and with the help of his wonderful wife, he did them all. A trip to Yellowstone with the whole family and a hot air balloon ride at dawn were just some of the gifts and surprises his wife made happen for him against all odds and just weeks before he died.

Humor had always been a major part of Tim's life, and this did not change now. He went off to the funeral home alone one afternoon to make his final arrangements. He was a University of Florida graduate, after all, and wanted to be sure that the blue and orange school colors would line his casket. He arrived home while I was visiting and came in the door laughing at the funeral director's shock at the plan he had in mind. He said he just blew the poor guy away.

Tim wanted to meet with the pastor of the Methodist church near his home and plan his own funeral so that his service would be a meaningful memory for his family. He wanted it to be upbeat, not sad, with happy music. He wanted it to reflect all that was most important to him in life. He wanted the memory of it to be a good one for his girls and comforting for the wife he loved so much. He set an early morning appointment with a wonderful minister he came to know and love in his remaining days. He could not have chosen a more compassionate man than Pastor Gene to discuss the important things in life, and together they planned the service that would celebrate his young and very full life. Pastor Gene told us later that as they chose the readings and music for the day and shared communion, he had never been more aware of the presence of Christ.

Tim remained as busy as his illness would allow, trying hard to put as many things in good order as he could, and not wanting to concentrate too much on what was really happening to him. Although he was a realist at heart, the pain he knew his wife and children would suffer in losing him was matched only by the heartache he felt in leaving them. One day out of the blue, Tim said to me, "I really don't want to die, you know, Trudy, but I wouldn't give anything in the world for this past year. I have never loved so well, and I have never known how to accept love like I do now."

One day when I stopped by for a visit, Tim made it clear that he wanted to talk privately, really talk. "I'm losing control," he said, "please help me. I'm afraid I'm going to get angry with the girls or Rebecca one day, like I did when I dropped the soap in the shower this morning. I just lost it and I couldn't help myself. I couldn't bend down to pick it up." He spoke with so much anguish and sadness in his eyes, I thought my heart would break for him. "What can you do to help me?" he asked.

"I have nothing to give you that will change the physical things that are happening to you," I said to him. "But I think if we talk to God about them, He will help you in ways that I cannot. He knows everything that's happening to you, and only He understands what will make this time easier for you." Tim, sitting next to me on the sofa, simply nodded his head in agreement. "Do you want to pray together?" I asked.

"Yes, please," he responded.

"I'm Irish, you know," I said to him, "so can we hold hands?"

Reaching out, he simply took both my hands in his, wordlessly, and bowed his head.

"Heavenly Father, You promise when two or more people are gathered together in Your name, that Your Divine Son is always present with us. Lord, we take You at Your word. Lord Jesus, we ask You to be present here in this very room with Tim now. Please put Your loving arms around him and hold him close to Your heart and give him the peace that only You have to give. Above everything else, help him to see how much You love him, how close You are to him now, and how safe he is in Your care." We sat together quietly for a few minutes, then Tim went to his study to be alone. Rebecca and I quietly shared a cup of tea in the kitchen for the next half hour. She loved this man so much and would have given anything for this not to be happening to him now. But she knew she could change none of it for him. She was unbelievably brave.

As I was leaving, Tim insisted on walking me to the door, closing it behind him. "I have my peace now," he said quietly, looking me straight in the eye, "and nothing can take it away from me again." In every visit and phone call from that day until the day he died, Tim reminded me in very comforting tones that he had his peace. God had put a gentle and quieting hand on his soul now, and he knew it.

"Will you come back this weekend and take the girls for ice cream cones?" he asked. "Make it Saturday, OK?" I promised him I would be by on Saturday for this special outing, wondering to myself why he had named the day for ice cream cones.

Saturday arrived, and the girls were dressed and ready to go by midmorning. Tim reached with difficulty into his pocket for change for the ice cream cones.

"May I treat them today?" I asked him.

"OK, just this once," he said. "And take your time, Trudy, and thank you." He spoke softly as he kissed the girls goodbye, telling them to have fun and to be good. His eyes reflected clearly his understanding that his time was very near, and this time alone with Rebecca was all-important to him. The brave front of being "Daddy" for them to the last was powerful to see and caused an ache in my heart too deep for words. When someone who is so close to their dying time looks at you with the complete knowledge that you know and they know they are dying, souls touch and are never the same again. Now, they would have their quiet time together, just Tim and Rebecca.

The ice cream store was a fun experience, and we chose wisely the flavors we wanted. We took our time there enjoying every last lick and got back in the car for the short drive home. "Can we stop in there?" the littlest one asked just as we passed the big cemetery on the right. *Does she really mean the cemetery?* I wondered. "Yes, please, can we go in now, and I'll show you where Daddy will be."

Without another word, and with my heart in my mouth, I turned into the beautiful cemetery, just off the main road. The girls jumped out of the car together and knew just where they were going.

"Daddy will be right there, by that big tree," one of the girls said, pointing to a beautifully mowed, lush green lawn beneath a towering tree. "See how pretty it is. The ducks are always in the water, and the sun shines here all the time." The two little girls stood side by side looking over the lake where their daddy would be buried. They were happy that it was so pretty and close to their house, so they could visit him often. Tim and Rebecca had come here with the girls to show them where Daddy would be. How unbelievably brave of two young parents to do such a touching and loving thing for their children. How natural it seemed to the little ones to talk about it with them—not easy, but oh so natural.

Tim died that evening, resting in Rebecca's arms, looking straight into her eyes and loving her until the very last minute. She was with him to the end, and that was the most important thing of all.

For those who are fresh from the Father's arms, like children are, death and transition seem more natural and not fraught with the fear that we develop as adults. These two little girls were lovingly prepared by both their parents for the loss they were about to experience. As heartbreaking as their loss was, this very special time of preparation left them a soft pillow of understanding they could not have known otherwise. This young and vibrant couple loved each other intensely, and although the pain of impending loss was too deep for words, they bravely loved and supported each other until there were no more days left to them.

# Jess

*"I think he sees Jesus."*

Jess, in his early seventies, had been married many times and had children and grandchildren he did not even know. Contacting his youngest daughter, he asked if he could come home to her house to die. The daughter he barely knew immediately said yes. There were lessons for all of us to learn. We watched this youngest daughter not only care for her dying father with love and tenderness but also teach her own family, by example, to do the same.

Jess was about to be loved in a way he had never known before and did not believe possible. There were many children in the home, but his six-year-old grandson, John, took charge. Putting a mat on the floor so he could sleep next to Grandpa's hospital bed and using a clothesline as a make-believe door, he transformed the family room into Grandpa's new bedroom. John seldom left Jess's side, and if and when he had to be away from the house, he would always run first thing to check on Grandpa when he got home. The tender bond that quickly established between them reminded all of us that it is often a little child who leads us.

Jess was declining rapidly with a diagnosis of stomach cancer that had spread to other parts of his body. He thought and spoke about all of his ex-wives and the children and grandchildren he created but did not even know. He had, like all of us, things he wished he could do over again, and he confessed his sorrow often to those around him.

The word got out somehow that Jess was "home" and dying. Many family members from near and far found their way to him for a visit. Half-brothers and half-sisters met for the first time and had great fun trying to match just who came from which family and how they were related. Working together, they provided the peaceful, forgiving, and loving setting that God wanted Jess to experience at this time in his life, and Jess was profoundly grateful for it all.

Why does it take us a lifetime to learn the lessons little John was teaching us? Why do we have so much trouble forgiving and loving those around us? When will we really learn that only God knows just what He puts in each of our baskets when we are born, and therefore no one else can judge our actions except Him? Wouldn't it be great if we all accepted each other exactly where we are and trusted God to do the rest? He only asks us to love like He does, and He sends us a precious child like John to show us how.

One afternoon while I was visiting, Jess asked, "How come I can see them already"—speaking about his parents who had died years earlier—"while I can still see you?" He asked the question very naturally, reflecting a newfound acceptance of the here and the hereafter. I explained to him that God was preparing to take him into heaven soon, and that while his soul was getting ready to leave his body, his body was not ready to let go just yet. Over many years of caring for dying patients, hospice nurses come to understand, in a very tangible way, that the body, soul, mind, and spirit are all intimately connected, and that God, who created all of us, is drawing the whole person. When each of these elements is attended to, then and only then is the person able to transition peacefully into the next phase of their life, which is their death.

Each day, John would sit close to Grandpa's bed, touching him gently and watching TV with him. Slowly but surely, Jess's life was ebbing away, but not before finding the unconditional, all-forgiving love he had been seeking his entire life. He found it all through John.

"How does he feel?" John asked moments after Grandpa died.

"You can touch him if you want to," I said as he reached out gently to feel his grandpa's face.

"What is in his eyes?" he asked.

"You can open them up and look to see if you want to," I said.

Slowly, John lifted himself up onto the bed, and opening Grandpa's eyes he said, "I think he sees Jesus!" This seemed very natural to one so young and untouched by the world's need to interpret everything. Grandpa was in heaven now, and it made good sense to John that he was looking at Jesus. Out of the mouths of babes oftentimes come gems.

Seeing that John was not yet ready to leave and wanted to spend more time with Grandpa, we left the room and closed the curtain, separating him from the rest of the house. About fifteen minutes later when I had completed all the funeral arrangements, I peeked around the clothesline that was his door, and there on top of the bed was little John, straddling his grandpa, with arms wrapped around his rotund belly, sound asleep.

# Johnny

*"But suppose I just don't believe
in Him, what then?"*

Johnny was a hard drinker and chain smoker. He had lived alone for a long time, separated from his only son, whom he now asked to take care of him. His son, whom he had left when he was a young boy, agreed. Johnny had very few soft edges, and now, diagnosed with inoperable lung cancer, he was even harder to please or make happy. He was angry and tired, and no amount of kindness or help was received well by him. For some reason that I do not fully understand, grouchy and seemingly mean-spirited people have always intrigued me. I think I always felt there had to be some good inside of them that not even they knew about, and I wanted to find it.

His son agreed to take care of his father at home for as long as it seemed safe to do so. He did exactly that. Being a local fireman, he knew all too well the dangers of older people living alone, and although he very seldom went out of town, he wanted to be sure of his father's safety if he did. As Johnny began to decline, he often forgot to take the medications that kept him both out of pain and breathing easier. But after he forgot to turn the stove off one too many times, the decision was made for him to enter a long-term-care living facility. He settled in quickly and seemed grateful to be well cared for there.

Johnny often said that he did not believe in God, but he brought Him up often in conversation, out of the blue and for no apparent reason. In the middle of talking about something entirely different, Johnny would angrily ask how smart people could believe in a God they could not see. He thought that those who believed were weak and dependent, and he had no time for them or their thinking. He would often say, "Here comes that God person," when I visited him in the nursing home, all the while giving me a big smile and a wink. I think he recognized the cross I wore as a symbol of something he did not understand, and he both wanted and did not want to know about it. Little did we know what God had in mind to tenderize this heart that was longing for something and someone it did not yet understand.

We developed a very sweet friendship over the next three or four months, both of us knowing his time was growing shorter. His son watched with great surprise as his father slowly but surely softened toward him, and although they did not actively talk about the heartfelt things, his son understood that he wanted to but just did not know how. It seemed enough for them both to communicate with a gentle nod or touch on the shoulder.

Johnny had been an avid smoker all his life and he remained so, even now. He could only light up and enjoy his cigarette outside the nursing home in the gardens. He would ask me from time to time to take him there in his wheelchair for a "smoke," which I did. But as he grew weaker, getting in and out of the wheelchair was too difficult for him. One day he asked if I would take him "one last time" to the screened porch where he was also allowed to smoke. I knew his time was near, and so did he. So we went.

Sitting quietly smoking his cigarette, he looked up at the wall facing him, and pointing to the famous picture of Jesus knocking on a door, he asked me what it meant. "The picture is of Jesus," I said, "and the door is your heart. Jesus is knocking on it. Tell me what you see in the picture that is different."

Leaning as close to the picture as he could get, he said, "There is no doorknob on the door. Why is that?"

"God is so gentle and tender with us, He will not force His way in," I said. "He wants you to open it from your side and invite Him in. The door has to be opened from the inside, by you. He only wants to come into your heart and make Himself known to you and take you to heaven with Him."

He did not seem a bit put off by my explanation but smiled a gentle and trusting smile as I wheeled him back to his room. "But suppose I just don't believe in Him at all, what then?" he asked. As I tucked him back in bed for the night, I suggested that he just tell God that he had never believed in Him and ask Him to please show him if He really exists. "Tell Him you're sorry for whatever you did wrong in your life, and ask Him to take you to heaven with Him, if that's where He is," I suggested.

He smiled as we said good-bye, both of us knowing it would be for the last time.

Here was a lonely, angry man who would have died alone if it had not been for a very forgiving and loving son who took him in when he needed him most. Here was a son who was able to put aside the hurts of the past and accept this father as he was and give him respect and care, withholding nothing. Here was a man who probably was looking for God all his life but did not know how to find Him. And here was God, in the wings all the time, wanting to comfort and love this one lost soul.

Johnny died in the early morning hours of the next day. The nurse called to say that he never moved after I left and simply went off to sleep peacefully. She asked me to notify his son, who was out of town, and asked if I would come by for his clothes and things since they needed the room right away for another patient.

Visiting the nursing home later in the morning, I passed through the porch where Johnny and I had sat the evening before. Not seeing the picture on the wall, I asked the nurse about it. She reacted with surprise, saying there had never been a picture of Jesus on that wall, and yes, that was the only porch at the facility, and yes, that was where he sat having a smoke with me the evening before. After carefully examining both the porch and the wall itself for nail marks or fading, I realized she was right. No picture had ever hung on that wall. Needless to say I was speechless, and so was she. Who can explain the awesome power of God?

# Margaret

*"I want to see every pretty
thing in my new home."*

Margaret was a ninety-year-old independent lady who had
lived by herself in the same small apartment for more than
fifty years. Frail and dying now, with a diagnosis of cancer of
the stomach, she wanted to remain in her own place to die,
having declined any other form of treatment for her disease.

When Margaret could no longer care for herself in a safe
way, her nurses convinced her to come to the hospice center
for her remaining days. She was none too happy to leave
her home of fifty years, but realizing it was not safe to stay
alone any longer, she reluctantly agreed. She quickly fell in
love with the beauty of the place and the people caring for
her there.

On the evening she was admitted, I received a call from a
social worker who told me that Margaret wished to see me
and an attorney to arrange to leave all her worldly possessions

to the care of hospice patients in the future. She wanted others to be cared for in this beautiful place and to experience the love she found there in one short day.

Time was very short for Margaret, and although I felt she probably had few worldly possessions, I arranged for her to see an attorney that day. As God would have it, the attorney's mother had lived in an apartment across the hall from Margaret for many years, so they had much to say to one another, which was of great comfort to her. This attorney was abundantly kind by nature, and just exactly what Margaret needed at this time in her life.

Arrangements were made within hours of her admission to leave all her worldly possessions for the care of others who would come to the hospice center as she had. Margaret asked to be taken by wheelchair on a tour of the center so that she could see "every pretty thing in her new home." The tour took the home health aide more than two hours, since Margaret wanted to stop at every picture along the way to see who had donated it, how it was acknowledged, and where it had been placed on the wall.

Before leaving for home that evening, I stopped by to see Margaret. She explained to me that although she had never believed in God in her lifetime, she was experiencing a very new peace in the people she saw around her, in their faces, in their words, and in their touch. "Is that what God is all about?" she asked. "When people say that God is love, is that what they mean?" She wanted to know why she had this new and comforting feeling, and I assured her that God would visit her here, Himself, and that He would make His presence known to her, in all the people He would put around her. "I feel His peace now," she said, "whenever I see you, and whenever the people taking care of me here look at me and smile, I know He must be close by."

Margaret lived a lifetime in this one day, settling into a new home, making arrangements with the attorney for her belongings, and coming to new insights about God and His love for her, in a very short period of time. I tucked her into bed before leaving and assured her again that she would have the most tender loving care here all night long, and that God Himself would remain as close to her as every person who attended to her needs. Margaret died in the early hours of the following morning, having nestled into her newfound home and being at peace with God and everything around her. It all happened in less than twenty-four hours.

How good God is to place His children in safe and compassionate surroundings, and to make Himself known to them with such simplicity and grace. He touched her soul and gave her peace through the attorney He sent to tend to her affairs and through the people He assigned to her care. Margaret too had a very generous heart and wanted so much for others to benefit from what little she had to share. The widow's mite is often a greater gift than one easily given by someone of great wealth. We were all the better for having known Margaret, even for this very short time.

Margaret's gift to hospice was two large Hefty bags left on the floor of my office the next day. In the bags were all the possessions she owned in the world. They consisted of old letters, photographs, a tiny family box with pins and mementos, a garter belt from the thirties, and one small, very old Bible inscribed by family members over the years.

After much investigation, I found a distant niece who had known this aunt in her youth and who was happy to receive Margaret's belongings. She was grateful to know that her aunt had died peacefully, surrounded by people who had tended to her needs and cared for her with compassion in the last days of her life.

# Katy

*"I always hoped I would see you
one more time before I died."*

"I know who you are," said the voice on the phone in the doctor's office that I called one afternoon. "You took care of my father many years ago." It took only a short time and very few words between us to reconnect and remember the fifty-year-old patient with the brain tumor who was cared for at home with wonderful children and a beautiful wife named Katy.

"My mom is in a nursing home now," the daughter said. "She's declining and is not doing well these days. Her one wish in life is to see you one more time before she dies. She's often spoken about when my dad was dying, and you were taking care of him. Do you think you can visit her one day soon? I don't think she has much time left." I promised to visit her the very next day, as I remembered Katy as such a loving and kind wife to her husband. She had cared for him with such simplicity and grace many years ago, and she was hard to forget.

I knocked on the door marked with her name and entered a darkened room at the nursing home early the next morning. "Katy, Katy," I called softly, to which a frail and whispering voice responded, "Yes, yes."

"This is Trudy," I said, moving slowly across the room and sitting on the edge of her bed. This beautiful, frail, elderly lady sat up at this early hour of the morning, with all of the energy she could muster. She reached out, and, opening her arms wide, she embraced me, rocking me back and forth like a baby. We stayed that way for a long, long time, just resting in the memories we shared so long ago at such a tender time in her life. "Oh, I can't believe it's you," she said. "I had always hoped I would see you one more time before I died."

We reminisced together, as if eighteen years had just slipped away and it was only yesterday. It was a joyful experience for both of us. We spoke about those days long ago, and her wonderful husband, and the tender, gentle last days of his life. The way she had cared for him, the makeshift bedroom they had created in the living room, her shaving him, and the many sweet things he had said to her at the end. The comfort and solace of remembering is impossible to describe, and she told me then, with great enthusiasm, how much she was looking forward to seeing him again. Katy died peacefully in her sleep, one week later, and I will be forever grateful to her daughter for asking me to visit her.

God does not ever work only one side of the track. In all the experiences of life, He enables both sides to learn and to grow from each other, if only we are willing to listen. In some mysterious way, He teaches every person what He wants him or her to understand and to know. With Katy, I learned about the depth of love people can have for one another, and the physical beauty God allows them in order to show His face to others. Katy's beauty came from deep inside, and it never changed. She was as beautiful then as I had always remembered her to be. She reflected all that is good and holy in the world. Katy knew what real love was all about, and she reflected that love all her life. I was grateful to have had the chance to remember her well.

Relationships forged during very special times in our lives are never broken. They remain strong and loving, reflecting good and faithful times shared by those whom God has made instant friends for His own purposes.

# Zach

*"He knows, he knows."*

He was only three years old, but he was dying. His young mother was devastated, and his dad, an officer in the navy, could not believe even for a moment that this was true. The pain surrounding the impending loss of a child is too hard to describe, but when this pain cannot be shared or talked about, each person suffers alone. Time was becoming very short for Zach, and the anxiety, fear, and anger experienced by everyone was both palpable and overwhelming.

Zach's dad found it impossible to give words to the impending loss or express himself in any way, and therefore was suffering alone. Zach's mom, having no one with whom to really share the intimacy of her loss, was essentially suffering alone as well. We needed to help this young family deal with what was soon going to be an overwhelming sorrow, and time was running out. His wonderful nurse, Kelly, placed a large roll of drawing paper in front of Zach and asked if he would draw a picture of what was happening to him. He was in his bed, with parents on either side, as he began to draw. A large ship emerged as only a three-year-old can draw. At the center of the ship was a woman with arms hanging by her sides and large tears falling from her face, onto her dress, and then onto the deck of the ship. At the far right was a stick figure of a man in uniform, with a hat and lots of colored buttons on his shirt. The line drawn down the center of his forehead reflected sadness and pain. In the far left corner of the large pad, a tiny boat was shown sailing away until it could be seen no more. Zach's dad began to cry. "He knows, he knows," he said. This little boy was telling his mom and dad what was happening to him, and he did not seem to be the least bit afraid, just anxious for them to understand. That day the floodgates opened wide with tears and kisses all around, allowing this young family time to prepare, as best it could, for the impending loss of this precious child.

He wanted to let his parents know what was happening to him, and he was finally able to do that, in a way they could understand.

His devoted nurse, who loved and cared for this young family and taught new hospice nurses many lessons with the gifts God had given to her, shared this story. She helped us all to hear and see in a whole new way and to develop the sensitivities and insights so important when caring for those who are dying.

# Eileen

*"Is it true that only Catholics can pray with Catholics?"*

"There is a patient down the hall who has a brain tumor and who is not able to speak," the young nurse said as she entered my office. "I think she wants someone to pray with her. Will you come with me?" It seems the patient was Catholic and someone had told her that "only Catholics can pray with Catholics." No amount of prodding on my part could convince her that God has an interdenominational heart and that she could easily pray with someone not of her own denomination on her own.

As I entered her room I found a lovely woman in her mid-sixties dying of a malignant tumor on her brain that left her weak on one side and unable to express herself. Her family explained that it had been her custom to attend church each day and to receive communion. She seemed to be trying to ask them for something now but was having great difficulty expressing herself, and they were not sure what she wanted of them.

I told Eileen that I went to church each morning too and that I would be happy to pray with her at the start of each day and to bring communion to her. Her face lit up like a light-bulb, and reaching up she pulled me by my jacket close to her face, smiling as best she could. It was evident to everyone in the room that this was what she had been asking for. The comfort and reassurance of Jesus Himself, which had been so important to her all her life, was even more important to her now that she was dying.

Eileen did not live many more weeks after our first meeting, but we met each morning to pray together and experience the presence of God in her life, talking about the Jesus she knew and loved so well. She was certain she would see Him soon face-to-face, and she looked forward to that time. She slipped away quietly in her sleep at peace in both body and soul.

A week or two after her death, a knock came at my office door, and a woman of thirty-five or forty was standing there. In her arms was a beautiful, old-world wooden cross of the crucified Christ. Introducing herself, she said to me, "We brought my mother to this beautiful place to give her body and her mind comfort, so she would not have any pain or be afraid. She found that here, surrounded by compassion and tenderness from the hospice staff. But you brought peace and healing to her soul, by visiting her and praying with her, and bringing communion to her in the mornings. I know that she would want you to have this." Handing me the beautiful cross she was holding, she explained that it had hung over her mother's bed for as long as she could remember. A family treasure she now wanted to share. Her gift could not have meant more to me, and it hangs in a special place in our home to this day.

The time spent with Eileen meant as much to me as it did to her. The gift of being present with a soul as God prepares its homecoming cannot be easily explained. It is so holy and so tender. You see firsthand the soul, as it is embraced by God Himself, snuggle down and find that little prepared corner where it can rest in Him.

The things that are most important to us in our lifetime remain most important to us as we are dying. In Eileen's case, being with her God meant everything to her, and saying the prayers most familiar to her brought her great comfort and peace. Her daughter's tender thoughtfulness was a reflection of the gift Eileen had passed on to her, that of a very generous spirit.

# William

*"Can you stop by for a cup of coffee this morning?"*

William was ninety-two years old, and we had been friends for more than twenty years. His wife had been my patient then, and we had become "Can you stop by for a cup of coffee?" friends ever since. Independent all of his life, William remained so and continued to live alone following the death of his wife. He moved from place to place as the need arose, working on his plans to build another airplane and steering clear of any conversation with anyone who said he should do otherwise.

But as the years passed and William, diagnosed with lymphoma, began to decline, it was evident that he could no longer stay at home safely. No amount of convincing could get him to move in with his two sons, who lived out of town. "They have their own lives," he would say to me, "and I have mine, and I don't want to disturb any of it."

After much conversation over a period of weeks, and with his permission, I called his sons and asked if they would come for a visit. They came immediately. The older son, with whom he stayed in close contact, handled all of his personal affairs. The younger son, whom he loved equally, he had not seen in some time. They both had families of their own, with all the challenges entailed in raising children. William had a tender heart for his grandchildren, some of whom had higher hills to climb than others. He spoke about all of them often.

They all agreed, except William, that moving into a place where he could have help if he needed it was essential. I knew for certain that William should be admitted into the hospice center, but I was the only one thinking in those terms, so that didn't happen. Settled quickly into an assisted living residence, William was able to spend some really good and meaningful time with his sons, especially the younger one with whom he had not been as close. They were very grateful now to be together and to share some good and happy times.

Although I saw very clearly that William was declining and his time on earth getting shorter, any discussion of having end-of-life care would not be heard by any of them. Dad was going to live a good long time now, in their estimation, and that was that. Getting him settled in and safe was all-important to them, and that is exactly what they accomplished. They hovered around him, bought him a new flat-screen television, put all his favorite things around him, and celebrated his new "digs" with him.

William adapted to his new surroundings, and his sons went home. The younger one, with whom he had been able to spend some very special time, died in less than a week of a massive heart attack. The shock to William was enormous, but there are no words to describe the gratitude he expressed for the time God had given him with this particular son.

William often told me that he had only ever felt comfortable with two clergymen in his life. One was a priest whom he had known in WWII. The other one was Father Seamus O'Flynn, who had tended to his wife when she was dying and who had presided over her graveside service years ago.

He spoke about Father O'Flynn with great affection and wanted to see him again. "Not immediately," he said, "I will tell you when." Within just a few short weeks William began to decline rapidly and asked me to call Father O'Flynn. He came to visit that very day, and they spent several very happy hours together. William told me later they were peaceful hours, filled with good talks and comforting words. He was convinced now that God loved him and had forgiven him any transgressions he had made and accepted him just as he was. He was finally at peace in a way that I had not seen in twenty years.

During the lunches we shared over the years at Epping Forest on the grounds of the old DuPont estate, William and I had often spoken about his desire for me to be with him when he was dying. We had reviewed the possibility of his coming to my house in the last few weeks of his life, but he was never one to want to impose. He was comfortable with the knowledge that he would not be alone and that we would be friends to the end. He assigned great humor to these "end of the line" discussions, and we often wondered what people around us would think if they could hear what we were talking and laughing about.

William was not in his new surroundings long before he began to decline rapidly. We spoke on the phone often and visited several times a week. One week, after we had visited for three days in a row, something or someone nudged me to visit him again, later in the afternoon. William was weak and nauseated when I got there and not able to keep anything down. He was sitting up straight in his chair, looking very pale and trying to be ever so brave. I knew his time was very close. With the help of his hospice nurse I tried everything I could think of to alleviate his symptoms, but to no avail. Nothing was working. Not wanting to leave him alone in such a weakening state, I promised to stay the night. I spoke with him about the possibility of getting him a room at the hospice center if things did not improve. He was sure that was not necessary and simply said no. We both knew that in the past I had promised to take him home with me at the end, which I was more than willing to do. But I explained that since we could not get his nausea controlled and make him feel better, going to the hospice center might be the best thing to do. Staunchly independent to the end, he let me know clearly that he did not think he was that sick and simply did not want to go.

We settled in for the night, just sitting quietly holding hands. A friend who had been extremely kind to him over the years and to whom he was most grateful stayed close by, gathering things together for him as he asked. A few hours passed with no letup of the nausea and vomiting, and William was getting weaker. After a few more hours he finally relented and allowed me to arrange for a room with a hospice nurse who had held one open at the center all night long.

It was a sight. William sitting up on the stretcher, arms folded across his chest, dressed to the nines, and stating loudly to the nurse on duty that he was "just fine, thank you!" and didn't need "all this attention." Since I had been speaking to her over a period of hours, telling her how close he was to his dying time, she could hardly believe what she saw and heard when he came down the hall on the stretcher.

The hospice staff tended to his needs immediately with IV fluids and medication. When he finally became comfortable and admitted that he was happy just to be there and feel better, I left, telling him that I would see him first thing in the morning. For twenty years, William and I had a pact that I would be with him when he was dying, and for all the world, this seemed to be the time. I felt a little guilty leaving him now, but he looked so at peace, and I knew he would be tenderly cared for there for the night. I phoned his son to tell him of the change in his dad, and he said he would arrive first thing in the morning. He was on his way immediately.

Arriving early the next morning, I found William sleeping peacefully, his son talking quietly with the nurse at the foot of his bed. Everything seemed to be in good order, the way William always liked things to be. There is so much truth in the saying that people often die the way they have lived. William was a quiet, peaceful man, not given to excitement or disarray. He valued his own space, his own thoughts, and doing things his way. This was his time to die, and he was doing it in exactly the same way he had lived, quietly, no fanfare or fuss. It was so like him.

With only minutes left to his life, I took his hand gently into mine and whispered in his ear, "Everything is in good order now, nothing left to be done. Why don't you just let go now, and go on to God. He loves you very much, and He is waiting for you." Taking three gentle breaths, he died.

What a lovely man William was, and what a joy and privilege it was to have been his friend. The laughs we shared, the secrets told and held close to the heart, the trust of two good friends sipping a cup of coffee together, and the lovely times spent at our elegant lunches over the years! How do you put a value on such things? The memory of him and the happy times we spent together is a gift I will treasure forever.

I must say here as well that a wonderful physician, Dr. Doug Johnson, whom William trusted implicitly, allowed William to speak candidly about his disease and the path it would take. These open discussions enabled William to play an important role in all the decisions that were made for his care. He liked and respected this physician so much, and the relationship they had helped William remain the dignified and private man he had always been. They shared other interests as well, such as flying and plane building, and William often spoke with great affection about his doctor. Physicians who are "human" and allow their patients to remain "real people" even when they are dying play an enormous role in a person's ability to die well. This special physician did just that.

# Lorrain

*"Every year in February one
yellow rose blooms."*

Lorrain was just six weeks old, born with a heart defect that
could not be repaired. She had been taken home to be cared
for by her young parents until she died.

Young professionals can handle anything, right? Aren't
they supposed to be able to fix any problem, mend any defect,
and make it all right?

Not so. As much as these young parents wanted to make
her better, this beautiful little girl could not be fixed. Saddened and unbearably helpless, her parents loved and tenderly cared for her until she quietly went to sleep for the last
time in her own home.

"Can we put her in bed with us and sleep with her tonight?" they asked the nurse who was caring for her. "Yes,
of course you can, and I will come by early in the morning
to bathe and dress her with you." Together they would drive

her to the funeral home to be laid out in her christening gown and placed in her little white bassinet to be buried.

On the way to meet the young family the next morning, the nurse stopped at a florist to pick up some beautiful yellow roses to give to them. She did not know why she stopped for the flowers, she just felt moved to do so. The parents, seeing the roses, smiled. How could this lovely nurse know that this young couple would see the yellow roses as a sign of God's intimate love and care for them? They knew now that Lorrain was safe in His care.

Pure faith, when seen firsthand, up close, and in the most tragic of circumstances, takes your breath away. In the face of the tremendous loss of a newborn baby girl, this young couple could find solace in the gift of roses, only because they had the faith to believe. Faith forged and practiced throughout life seems to be that soft place on which to rest when tragedy comes our way. The lessons learned by those of us on the periphery of these life experiences are forever etched in our minds and hearts. They are gifts of faith shared wordlessly by those God places in our care. Who is the gift and who is the gift giver?

As I was telling this story several years later at a large gathering, a young woman came to the stage to speak with me. "I am Lorrain's mother," she said to me, "and there is more to that story. A friend sent a beautiful rosebush for our garden when Lorrain went to heaven," she explained. "And every year, on the anniversary of her death in February, a lovely rose blooms." She thanked me for keeping her daughter's memory alive in the telling of the story. I don't think she could possibly have any idea just how powerful that experience was for others to hear. Over the years of telling that story, I have had many parents come forward to share their own very personal experiences of losing a child, and finding comfort in an unexpected way just as these young parents did.

# *Joel*

*"This is where God really lives."*

Joel was only fifteen years old. He had been battling cancer for more than five years and was now losing the fight. Wonderful parents, who loved him dearly, had not raised him in the church. They were frantic now, wanting Joel to know God personally. The parish priest was patient and kind with Joel, and understanding of his parents' need to "get everything right." He spent time talking with him about God and heaven and tried as hard as he knew how to help them all come to some understanding of the importance of this young life and now the meaning of his death.

Joel had a small bedroom where he spent a great deal of quiet and resting time. His bed was next to a window that was very narrow but at least eight feet high from the ceiling to the floor. He had looked out of this window for hours at a time over the last several years. One day when I was visiting him, I asked him to tell me what he saw there that interested him so much.

"This is where God really lives," he said to me quietly. He told me how he watched the bark fall off the large tree outside his window, year after year, and explained how it became part of the mulch when it fell to the ground. He told me about the squirrels and birds and other critters he saw there, and how busy they all were eating and fixing their nests with parts of that tree. He said that he would watch a tiny leaf sprout out of the dark brown, dead-looking mulch in the spring, and then in a short time produce a beautiful flower. He spoke about how beautiful the rain was when it fell onto the canvas of his window, and how it fed all the unseen things beneath the mulch. He said, unlike the rest of us, that he loved to see the leaves drop off the tree in the fall because he could look forward to their becoming newly green every spring, making the tree beautiful again. "How can people see all this and still not believe in God?" he asked. "It's really so simple."

The lessons Joel taught us about the tree reminds us that God is constantly nurturing every living thing through the daily gifts of sunlight and rain, that He brings beauty and understanding out of the darkness and peace in the midst of heartache and sorrow, and that He makes the promise of new life to all who believe in Him. We all recognized a simple, living, breathing insight and understanding of God in this young boy. Joel knew Him better than we all did, and we decided easily and quickly to sit quietly with him by his window and learn from him that "this is where God really lives."

A little child will often lead us, if only we will get out of our own way and just watch and listen. God had given Joel an understanding of life and beauty that most people spend a lifetime trying to find. He knew when He created him that Joel would have a short earthly life. God promised He would make things known to the simple, only to confuse the wise. I don't know about you, but I'd much rather be the "simple" one whom Jesus speaks about, rather than the "wise" one who remains blinded by his or her own sense of intellectual importance. Lord, please help us all.

# Sam

*"He looked at her with about as much love
as I have ever seen in one man's eyes."*

Could life get any better than Sam and Betty had it? Second time around was a gem for the both of them. The life they shared was fun to watch, since they were such opposites: she, a soft and graceful beauty on his arm at the opera as he smiled all the way down the aisle. He, an avid fisherman and outdoorsman who loved the rough and tumble of everyday life with his buddies. Often he would go out on the boat for a good day of fishing with his friends and she would crinkle her nose and say, "I don't do fish" and they would laugh. They were so much fun to watch and to be around.

People of opposite backgrounds, experience, and tastes frequently are drawn to each other. I think somehow we all know that there is a part of us not fully fleshed out, and it is only through others that we become completely whole. That is true of friendships, marriages, and everyday family dynamics. Love makes those times possible. That was certainly true with Sam and Betty.

And then Sam was diagnosed with terminal cancer. It came on very suddenly and progressed quickly, with little time to prepare. It was not a good diagnosis, and it would not be long before the cancer took his life. You could be sure though that they would face it together, in their lovely beachfront home on the ocean, until the end.

Betty called one Sunday afternoon. "Sam doesn't look good to me," she said. "Will you come out to the beach to see him?" Fifteen minutes later, I was greeted by a beautiful but worried Betty and a sleeping Sam. Moving closer to the bed, she whispered softly to him, "Wake up, look who's come to see you." Very slowly he opened his eyes, and turning his head toward her, he smiled. When he turned his head to look at me, his eyes were filled with awareness and gratitude. His thoughts were vividly reflected there. He had been waiting for someone to come by. He did not want the love of his life to be alone; she wasn't now, and you could see the great relief on his face. He looked at her with more love than I have ever seen in one man's eyes, and turning to her he smiled and simply closed his eyes and died. Betty was so touched by the gentleness of his leaving, but she had taught him well about that "soft way" that was so much a part of who she was. They were together until the end, just as it should be.

# Madeleine

*"Oh, ma mère."*

Sixty-eight years old when she retired as my husband's executive secretary, Madeleine called to ask when she could start as my full-time volunteer secretary at hospice.

French Canadian by birth, never married, disciplined and determined, she had helped start and run large corporations for many years. She loved hard work and success and had no patience whatsoever with incompetent or lazy people. The work she accomplished, the responsibilities she handled, the speed and efficiency that were so much a part of her everyday life, were impossible to keep up with. She was, as I told her often, my hands and my feet, my brain and my heart on any given day. Fearlessly protective of my time and energy, she made possible every advancement at our new hospice program during her seven years of service to that organization and to me personally.

She arrived each day promptly at nine in the morning and left at exactly four each afternoon. She remained at her desk throughout the day and enjoyed her standard container of yogurt with a cup of coffee for her lunch. She never ate between meals and could not be tempted with even the sweetest of candies. She loved her raspberries and chocolate for dessert and sat as straight as anyone I have ever seen before or since.

She heard the stories of patients and families when they were in my care, and I often caught her just quietly listening to my phone conversations with them. She marveled at the naturalness of the dying process and the repetitiveness of the theme of God's redeeming love in each person's life. She especially liked meeting some of the patients in my care and hearing them tell of their personal experiences with Him in their own words.

"What will happen to me when I am dying?" she asked one day out of the blue. "When I get sick, what will we do?" Startled by the question, I told her that first we would talk about it honestly, the way we always did, and then, "You will come and stay with us until you die."

"Fine," she said, end of discussion, never to be brought up again. Somehow, on some level, she knew her time was coming, and it was so like her to want to have things in proper order.

Madeleine had given so much to so many all her life. She had played a major role in the early years of growing the local hospice, making the work we all did there easier by her experience, presence, determination, and nonstop support. And now it all came full circle. The teacher and caregiver now being taken care of by those she helped the most. "We could never have done any of this without you, you know," I would tell her when reviewing the accomplishments and growth of hospice. And she would sit up straight and reply with a big smile, "I know, I know." What you give away in life always comes back to you in one way or another. She had given so much all her life, and she received back in the end everything she needed and wanted most. God, who created us all and knows us well, sees to it.

About a year later, I started to see some changes with Madeleine: she was a little slower walking, a little more weary, a little less able, but still coming to work daily to help me.

"Madeleine fell in the parking lot," one of the nurses said to me one afternoon. "But she wouldn't let me help her up; she just dusted herself off and drove away." I quickly called one of my sons and asked him to rush to her condo and be waiting for her when she got there. As I suspected, she could barely get out of the car. A few hours later, I stopped by to see her; she was sitting at the kitchen table, having her usual late afternoon refreshment. "Let me see you get up," I asked, knowing full well she could not. A quick visit to the emergency room under duress, and Madeleine was instantly admitted. She had no broken bones but was obviously in congestive heart failure, complicated by her emphysema. Five days later, with discharge papers signed, Madeleine was set to go home to her two-story condominium with bedrooms upstairs. A quick conversation with her physician helped him to know that we needed to devise a new plan.

"I am going home tomorrow," she said, "to your house. Ken said so." Ken, our youngest son, knew Madeleine well and had been to her home on a number of occasions. He had stopped by to see her that afternoon at the hospital and without any conversation with anyone else had simply told her that she could not go home alone and would come home to us instead. And so she did.

Madeleine had her own room, with a monitoring system that could pick up her smallest movements and sounds. She tested it each night until she was sure I could make the distance from our room to hers in less than sixty seconds. She settled in easily, eating what she wanted, becoming weaker each day, but feeling ever so safe and happy.

I would not take a million dollars for the time we had together those several weeks and the fun and laughs we shared. On one particular day, I was sitting in the living room, where I could see her resting in bed. We had an agreement that she would not get out of bed without calling for help, but on this particular day she did not remember that. Suddenly, I saw her sitting up and then standing. It was as if it was all happening in slow motion as I raced to her room. Getting there just as she was going down to the floor, I decided to hold her tight and go down gently with her. There we were, the two of us, face-to-face on the floor, laughing out loud.

A call to my son, who was showering in the next room, brought him running to us, soaking wet, with a towel at his waist. He quickly told me to get up and out of the way, and, straddling Madeleine, he began to gently lift her up from the floor. There she was, feisty as ever, looking straight up his towel and laughing. "Good to see you again, Ken," she said. To which he replied, "This is no time for humor, Madeleine." She could make you laugh at so many things and found humor in almost any circumstance. Even now, on the floor, unable to get up by herself, she was laughing.

One afternoon as I was leaning toward her, fluffing her pillows, she reached up to touch my face and said, "Ma mère, ma mère," which means "my mother, my mother." She was speaking in the language of her youth, and I reminded her that although she had taught me many things in the years we worked together, French was not one of them. In one of those inexplicable ways that God allows to happen, Madeleine was experiencing her mother through me, and she seemed so excited at seeing her. How comforting, I thought, that God, who knows us so well, would enable her to experience this at this tender time in her life. In some way that I do not understand, I think we are all interconnected, splintered into finite pieces of the whole, and it is only through each other that we find ourselves.

Monsignor Mort Danaher, a close friend of Madeleine's for forty years, came by that evening to see her. They looked back with fond memories on the good times they had shared, and the laughter in that room was wonderful to hear. Father blessed her and gave her communion. When he asked me to give her something to drink, I simply handed her the glass next to the bed, not realizing it was a scotch and water. We guessed that might have been a first for the Lord.

Madeleine was very peaceful when Father left, and she went off to sleep with a smile on her face. She was contented that she had been with her lifelong friends and that she had received communion. Madeleine died peacefully at two in the morning, happy to be where she wanted to be, safe, loved, and in charge of everything to the end.

# Hannah

*"OK, I'm going, don't rush me."*

She was a forty-one-year-old mother with a very loving husband and a three-year-old daughter, but life had not been easy for Hannah. Her parents had died years earlier in a car crash, and Hannah, at seventeen, was left to raise her three younger sisters. The girls were as close as any four people could be and had grown up nurturing and protecting one another.

Now Hannah, so young and lovely, with a husband who loved her dearly and a precious three-year-old to raise, was dying. She, like her sisters, had a strong Christian faith, and she knew well that heaven was waiting for her. Still, she so badly did not want to leave them. Hannah lived every day to the fullest, with a very joyous spirit and a house filled with family, friends, and children. Good food was always around, and in spite of the enormity of this impending loss, this family exuded happiness.

Hannah's sisters spent lots of time with her—bathing her, fixing her hair, painting her fingernails, and tenderly covering her frail body with creamy lotion. They were doing for her now all the things she had done for them when they were little, and she reveled in every minute of it. Oftentimes when I visited Hannah, I would find her and all her sisters piled up in the bed together. I am sure it was just that way when they lost their parents years before and only had each other to love and rely on. It was very sweet to watch them love her in this way now, and her husband seemed to understand it all perfectly. He was so unselfish in his sharing of Hannah with them and reflected a very tender understanding of their closeness and need to be with her now.

Hannah had loved everyone and everything so well all her life. Now, as she was getting ready for her eternal reward in heaven, she was being loved equally well. You always seem to get back in abundance what you have given away during your lifetime, and that was happening for Hannah now. You can be sure her sisters gave back to the three-year-old she was leaving behind the same love she had given to them so long ago in full measure. They were, for her, what Hannah had been for them when they too were left without a mother. How often do we think about Jesus's words "love one another as I have loved you"? If only we could understand and practice them as well as Hannah did, I think the world would be just as God had planned it to be.

Hannah was getting weaker every day, and she rested often. Her room was filled with friends and family who loved her very much and whose lives she had made better along her short journey. Church friends, neighbors, relatives, and all those she had touched in some way were with her now. I think I will never forget her last day on this earth, with her husband kneeling on the floor beside her, and her daughter's little head resting in her lap. Her sisters had all climbed into the bed with her, encouraging her to "go on to heaven, Hannah, go on, just let go." To which Hannah quietly replied, just as she was dying, "OK, OK, I'm going; don't rush me." And she left.

# Frederick

*"If I saw Jesus like you did, would I cry too?"*

A neighbor, whom I did not know well at the time, met me on the front lawn as I got home from work one evening. She explained that she had an uncle in Boston who lived alone and had recently been diagnosed with a terminal illness. She said that she and her mother would like to take care of him and asked if I would help him get the care he would need if she arranged to bring him to our city. I immediately assured her that I would be happy to do so, to which she replied, "Oh good, because I gave his doctor your phone number." I loved it. Needless to say, in the ensuing years, she and I have become good friends.

Frederick was admitted into the hospice center within a week or two of his arrival in Jacksonville, and I had the joy of visiting him there every day. He was a magnificent-looking man, about seventy-eight years old, very elegant, with a naturally graceful demeanor. His hair was as white as snow, and his eyes were electric blue. As you entered his room, you were struck by the classical music playing day and night, freshly cut flowers everywhere, and greeting cards hanging from every slat on the louvered blinds. It was obvious that he was well-known and much loved. Frederick was extraordinarily well-educated with a background in philosophy and religion, and he had to say but a few words for you to fully understand that. He was a thinker, a deep thinker, about all the most important things in life, and he exuded the manners of a wonderfully genteel man.

One day when I stopped by for a visit, Frederick was sobbing. I sat quietly near his bed asking if there was something I could do for him. He simply shook his head and sobbed even harder. "Tell me what it is," I said. "No, no, no," he would say, "just sit here with me." This experience repeated itself many times over the next few weeks, and each time I found him in this way, I simply sat with him until he became tired and fell asleep. One day he said to me, "I have had an experience, and I will tell you about it one day, not now, not yet, but one day." That was all he said.

A few weeks later as I was leaving for home, I stopped by to say good night. This time Frederick was crying very, very hard. Looking up at me, he said simply, "Sit down." I sat down. He cried and cried quietly for a long time, and I just held his hand without saying a word. Finally he looked at me and said, "Do you remember my telling you about an experience I had that I would tell you about later on? Well, I am going to tell you about it now." He proceeded to tell me that Jesus Himself had come into this bedroom, here at the hospice center. Gesturing to a corner of the room, he explained that He had stood "right there," near the foot of his bed. He said Jesus's presence had filled the room with the most incredible sense of compassion, beauty, and forgiveness he had ever seen. He spoke of the love and tenderness he saw clearly reflected in His eyes, and the awareness he felt of being loved deeply, just for himself. Frederick spoke quietly, in awesome tones, and with an insightful and graceful manner about this very personal experience. He wanted to be sure I understood every word that he was saying.

"If I saw Jesus like you did," I asked, "would I cry too?"

"Oh yes," he replied.

"Why would I cry?" I asked him.

"Because He is so beautiful," he said, "and because He loves us so much and forgives us all our sins. He wants us to let Him love us and wants us to be free to love Him too, just as we are."

We spoke for a long time after his sharing this wonderful experience with me. I thought for all the world that he wanted me to get it right so as to be able to share it with others, as I am doing now. With all the education and experience Frederick had in life, and with all the knowledge others saw in him, Frederick, like all of us, simply did not know the depth of love God had for him. The hole in his heart was filled to capacity in the last hours of his life.

How do you explain these magnificent experiences that God allows His children to have? Who else but the One who created us all and loves us so intimately would know what each of us needs to be able to run home to Him the way a small child runs to his father after a long day of playing with its falls and scrapes and hurts? That, after all, is what we do at the end of our lives. We run home to the Father who made us, realizing all we have done and not done with our lives, trusting that He who knows our repentant hearts so well will read there the story of our lives and love us dearly anyway.

Early the next morning when I arrived at work, I stopped in to see Frederick. The nurses who had cared for him the evening before said he had gone off to sleep last night and had not really responded yet today. It was obvious that he was now resting in God's love and preparing to go home to Him, unafraid. He remained that way all day.

When I left for home that evening, I told him good-bye and thanked him for allowing me to be his friend, saying that God often allows people to become "instant friends" for reasons that we do not understand. He simply smiled, his eyes still closed, letting me know he had heard and agreed. When I arrived home twenty minutes later, my husband said the hospice center had called to say Frederick had just died.

# Ira

*"Large tears were flowing gently
from his closed eyes."*

"Please take this address down and stop by to see this patient right away," came the call from the hospice office one afternoon at about five o'clock. There was no information to speak of since the patient had just been admitted into the program that morning, and no file had yet been set up on him. His name was Ira, and his wife had called and asked that a nurse stop by this afternoon to see him. Was my heart in the right place at this hour of the day? No way. I was tired after seeing dying patients all day long, and I just wanted to go home, feed my family, and get into bed. This was not to happen, and I drove around in the evening rush hour, not in a happy mood, to find the high-rise apartment building where Ira and his wife resided. I tell you about my own weakness and bad attitude just to show you how God works both sides of the tracks in dealing with His children, comforting those He wants comforted and correcting those He wants to correct all within the same experience.

As I rang the doorbell a short time later, my heart was still not in a good place. An elderly woman answered the door, announcing that her name was Ruth and that she needed to go to temple right away to make "arrangements." With that, she flew past me and out the door.

*Who is Ira?* I wondered. *What is his diagnosis and status?* Since he had just been admitted into the program a few hours earlier, there were no records on hand to review. Wandering around a rather large apartment with very high ceilings and multiple rooms, I finally found Ira. He was a very tall, thin man, and he was resting quietly in bed, eyes closed, with shallow respirations and a pulse that was barely palpable.

I looked around a large room whose walls were covered with dozens of photographs, awards, letters, and pronouncements from dignitaries, presidents, and CEOs. This was who Ira was, a very famous man of great accomplishment and many successes. He was known to many, many people and had apparently been highly esteemed in his profession during his lifetime.

Sitting down on a chair next to his bed, I took his hand and held it gently in mine. "I see that you have lived a very full and productive life," I said to him, all the while praying that God would give me the words this gentle soul needed. "I see all that you have accomplished, and it seems that those whose lives you have touched thought very highly of you." Starting at one end of the room I reviewed each and every award, letter, and recognition reflected there, reading from each one until I had covered the entire room. In reading them out loud I could see the canvas of his life painted very clearly. I learned about where he had started working in the 1920s and 1930s, and how he had progressed from entry-level positions to leadership roles in those very same companies. Many professionals with whom he had worked along the way acknowledged all he had done for them and all he had accomplished.

Ira never opened his eyes during the hours it took to read all the accolades that reflected his very successful life. In some way he already knew that this part of life was ending. With his respirations slowing down and his color changing, I began to speak to him about how much God loved him, not really knowing anything about his belief system, only that he was Jewish and he was dying. "Your God is the God of Abraham and Isaac and Jacob," I said to him. "Their Father is your Father and mine as well. I know my God by the name of Jesus; He is the one the Father sent to bring us safely back home to Him." Hearing his wife coming in the door, I told him that I would be leaving now but would pray for him and call to check on him in a little while.

Ira had not moved at all in the few hours that I stayed with him. There was no movement on his part that gave me the idea he had heard anything that was said, but just as I was about to stand up and move away from the bed, he squeezed my hand tightly and would not let go. Surprised, I looked quickly to his face only to see large tears flowing from his still-closed eyes. In moments like these you see the hand of God most tenderly touch His children. In His own way and in His own time, He makes Himself known, and it is best to step back and watch and recognize what He is showing us.

I held Ira's hand tightly until his wife came into the room. She explained that everything was in good order, and she seemed relieved to have gotten the necessary arrangements made.

I excused myself, giving his hand one last, gentle squeeze, and headed to the office less than ten minutes away. When I arrived there the receptionist said that Ruth had just called to say that Ira had stopped breathing and had died. She seemed totally peaceful when I spoke to her shortly thereafter, saying that putting everything in order was all-important to Ira and she was happy she could do this last thing for him. I hung up the phone, knowing full well that God had ministered to Ira that afternoon and had taken the opportunity to minister to me as well.

# Aunt Helen

*"George, do you know a priest who will come to see me?"*

She was ninety-nine years old, blind and deaf, living in a retirement home in south Florida. She called my husband to see if we would go down to see her and think about bringing her to be with us in Jacksonville. Not in our own home, she said, just somewhere nearby so we could look in on her and visit her from time to time. Although she was legally blind, she could recognize voices, and if you got up real close to her and raised your voice, she could make out some of what you said. Aunt Helen was my husband's aunt on his father's side, and he had very fond memories of her when he was a young boy and their families did things together. We drove down to see her within days of her call, and although she was thin and frail and bedridden most of the time, she exuded great enthusiasm when we walked into her room. She said she knew it was George just as soon as she heard his voice in the hall, and she cried when she gave us a hug. She had been in a car accident while her ninety-five-year-old girlfriend was driving, and upon discharge from the hospital had been admitted into a nursing home to recover. The social worker on staff at the hospital determined that Aunt Helen could no longer live alone. For someone who had always called the shots in her own life, this did not feel good. She was frightened and alone there, and although her "girlfriends" visited her as often as they could, it just was not the same for her.

We spoke at length about what it would take to get everything arranged, selling her belongings, giving things to special friends, looking into her insurance coverage, finding a nursing home that could take her, as well as moving her up to Jacksonville as fast as we could. We visited for most of the day, promising to go back home and prepare for her arrival as soon as we could arrange everything. At this stage in life, especially when you are blind and deaf and in a strange place, everything that you want to happen seems to move in slow motion, and nothing in this instance could be hurried. Many a heartbreaking call took place between Aunt Helen and us, so fearful was she that we were not doing all that we could do as fast as we could. Finally with my friend Jackie pulling strings with a friend of hers who ran a nursing facility nearby, we arranged for a lovely room within five minutes of our home. We took off early one morning for the five-hour drive to south Florida to drive her back to her new home ourselves.

What a sight! Here was Aunt Helen bundled up in her robe and pajamas, wrapped in a big comforter in the front seat so she could recline and still have lots of leg room. Cold drink in hand, catheter and bag hanging on the low level cigarette lighter, with music playing and laughter for the next five hours. Did I mention the eight or ten bags of nightgowns, dresses, slippers, robes, bed jackets, diapers, curlers, makeup bags, and food jammed into the trunk of the car? You could barely close the lid, and the only request she had all that time was for chocolate milkshakes at McDonald's three times along the way. George broke all speed limits, I must confess, and we laughed out loud at the prospect of any cop daring to stop us to discuss anything less important than getting Aunt Helen home with us under these circumstances.

We arrived at the nursing home late in the evening, entering like vagabonds wandering in from the desert. The nursing staff that had been told of our coming received us with open arms. Ever so quickly they put Aunt Helen to bed, reviewing her medication list, which we had in hand, and she settled in like a newborn baby safe at last in her mother's arms.

Aunt Helen expressed her gratitude daily, and the fulfillment of any wish as small as a special taste of liverwurst, a frankfurter, a root beer, or an orange popsicle was met with lavish praise and thanksgiving. It was a joy to visit her there, and the hospice team that looked after her seemed like angels straight from heaven to her.

Aunt Helen was a sweet soul who never intentionally hurt anyone. She was lighthearted and fun to be around, and even at ninety-nine she could make you laugh at the silliest things and best of all at yourself. She loved her brother and his children, and I can still see those little handmade birthday cards arriving in the mail when our boys were small, with three pieces of Beechnut gum taped inside. Although she never married, she loved everyone around her and accepted you just as you were, no questions asked.

We went away for a weekend of much-needed rest, with our friend Dianne, a hospice nurse, looking after her. In those two days, a big change took place, and in no time at all Dianne was able to arrange a bed for her in the hospice center. Beautiful blue comforters from Dianne's home covered her bed, and lovely white nightgowns from Dianne's own granny graced her thin, frail body when we returned home. Although she had not been a churchgoer during her lifetime, Aunt Helen had always been abundantly kind and generous. She asked George if he knew a priest who would visit her now, and of course Monsignor Mort Danaher and Father Greg Fay went immediately to her bedside, bringing comfort she had never known before. The nurses in the hospice center, as well as all the other friends I worked with, surrounded her like mother hens with gentle voices and soft hands until she fell off into that final and gentle good night.

We were so blessed from the arrangements made through Jackie's friend at the nursing home, to the staff that was prepared to help us at whatever hour we arrived, to Dianne's protective kindness in ministering to all Aunt Helen's needs in our absence. There was no stone left unturned on her behalf. The hospice staff did everything to ensure her comfort as well as her peace of mind. The priests who responded to her cry for help at this her last hour comforted her soul as well. We saw one reflection after another of the comforting and loving God who created us all so He could love us in just this way. It could not have been any better.

# Diane

*"What would you think if I told you
that God has chosen to heal my soul
and my spirit but not my body?"*

She was only forty-one years old when she was first diagnosed. She was five feet eleven inches tall and simply gorgeous. She had red hair, blue eyes, and a personality and zest for life that you could not keep up with. With a handsome husband whom she adored and three precious red-haired kids, life was so good for Diane.

She and I had become good friends more than ten years before when she came to a cosmetics party at my house. As she was leaving, I asked her to stop by some morning for coffee when she had the chance. The very next morning she was on my doorstep at eight, after dropping her kids at school. When I told her I didn't make coffee, she said that I should not have asked her to stop by for some. She reminded me that I had suggested the night before that bright red eyebrows did not look good with her bright red hair, so we made some coffee and became fast friends from that moment on.

We raised our little ones together, and since we had traveling husbands, we spent many a night making clothes on the floor in her basement, talking about life, our hopes and dreams and all our worries. Since I could not sew to save my life, she had me cut and pin while she stitched it all together. Between the two of us, we cranked out more shorts and shirts, jackets and dresses than any one person could ever do alone.

Upwardly mobile husbands had us moving away in lots of different directions, but always, always, we stayed in touch and thought of each other as best friends.

We spoke often about every aspect of life with all its joys and sorrows. Diane was a spiritual person and was on a search for a deeper relationship with God. We often shared our thoughts and understandings about His place in our lives and about how much He loved us. During challenging times in both our lives, she would come over to my house in the evening. Diane collected prayers that spoke to her heart and copied them on a legal pad. Diane would read these prayers during our time together. I knew that God was preparing Diane for something new and extraordinary that would matter very much to her and her entire family in the future.

A few years passed, and she called one day from Atlanta to say that she and her family were going to be accepted into the church in two weeks. She wanted all of us to be there with them for this very happy occasion for which God had been preparing her for a long time. She now entered into a new time in life of understanding and loving God more deeply, and this new and exciting experience would influence her husband and children long into the future. Years passed and children grew, and Diane was successfully selling real estate.

Then a phone call came. Diane had had a seizure of some kind and had fallen down while showing a house. Lots of tests, scans, studies, and worry ensued. She was, after all, so young and vibrant and happy. How could anything be wrong with her? But it was. She was diagnosed with cancer of the lung, which had spread to her spine and brain, and things did not look good. Experimental drugs, special diets, and anything and everything to try to slow the disease were to no avail.

"Turn on the TV quickly," she said in an early morning phone call. "There's a priest in Boston named Father Ralph D'Orio who has the gift of healing. Will you go there with me? We could meet in Atlanta and fly to Boston together, and Lisa [her daughter] will come too." In no time at all we found out the particulars of date, time, and place and arrived in Boston. We headed for the little church where Father D'Orio was speaking.

What a new experience for all of us! Hundreds of people crowded into the tiny church, with very sick children and family members in wheelchairs and on stretchers. The service began. In my prayers for Diane, I had asked God to put His arms around her and hold her. I begged Him to heal her and told Him over and over again that we would leave her at the foot of His cross, knowing that He loved her more than any of us could, and that we would trust in His care for her.

At some point, Father D'Orio asked that everyone who wished to be prayed for come to the front altar rail, telling him where in their body they had disease. One by one he laid hands on them, and for the first time in our lives, we saw what being "slain in the Spirit" meant as people fell to the floor, with volunteers breaking their fall. We were startled and amazed at what we saw, all the while Diane proclaiming loudly that she was not about to do anything so foolish as that. We assured her that we had not come this far only to have her not do as she was asked. Reluctantly she started down the aisle, and as Father approached her, he asked where her disease was. She explained that she had lung cancer, which had spread to her brain and now was everywhere in her body. He placed his hands first on her head, then on her chest and back, and stepping down from the altar he wrapped his arms around her as she rested her head on his shoulder. It was as if time stood still for all of us as we watched the priest pray over and embrace Diane. It was as if we were watching Jesus Himself touching and healing her. Father D'Orio then took both of Diane's hands in his and walked with her up the marble steps behind the altar, directly in front of the life-size cross. When he laid hands on her again and began to pray over her, she collapsed to the floor and remained there in a restful, unmoving position until everything ended more than twenty minutes later.

When she awakened and came walking down the aisle toward us, she smiled and said, "Did I do what I think I did?" She looked absolutely radiant and peaceful. By the next day we were heading for home, not really knowing what it all meant and what the future would hold for Diane.

She returned to the Caribbean Islands, where she was undergoing experimental therapies, but to little avail. She called to talk early one morning, just weeks after her time in Boston. "What would you think if I told you that God has chosen to heal my soul and my spirit through this experience but not my body?" she said.

"How does that feel to you?" I asked her.

"It feels right and I can accept it," she answered. "I am at peace about it." Diane seemed very accepting of this new understanding and enlightenment about her life, saying she would be going home to Atlanta soon, and we would talk more then.

Some people are bigger than life. They love with gusto, share with abandon, and trust with a fierceness that defies common sense. Her life, though very short in years, was as full of good times and fun as the lives of those who live twice that long.

The call came from Lisa one afternoon about a week later. Diane had gotten home from the islands but was now back in the hospital. She was a great deal weaker, and things did not look good. All her family was with her now. We left for Atlanta immediately, driving as quickly as we could in the hope that we would be able to see her one last time. It was not to be. Seeing a bright and beautiful shooting star ride across the sky at dusk, we stopped at a pay phone on the highway to call the hospital. Diane had just died, they said.

This beautiful and vibrant woman left lasting footprints on the hearts and minds of everyone who had ever known her. With her zany sense of humor, zest for life, and deep and abiding love for her husband and children, Diane created memories that have never faded even after more than twenty-nine years. Diane had an uncanny resemblance to Shirley MacLaine. To this day, friends and family have only to see a Shirley MacLaine movie to remember Diane well. To recall her hearty laugh, her rubbing her nose as she prepared to tell a joke, her letting them all know she loved them well is to remember Diane as if she were here just yesterday.

I am more than certain that the lives of her beloved husband and her three children have been filled with grace because of the gift of faith that was given to her years earlier by God. Today they all minister in one way or another in their church communities, which I am certain God had in mind when he led them to their new church home in Atlanta those many years ago.

# Grandmother

*"The tail boat is here."*

All of life is a circle. If you look back to the third chapter in this book you will find a story entitled "Grandfather." The time frame between that story and this one is twenty-two years. Grandmother's life from the time Grandfather died, when she was seventy, until she joined him in heaven at ninety-two was an adventure.

Ann Lamprecht was born in Germany early in the twentieth century. She came to the United States with her family by boat, owning little more than the clothes they wore. In those days survival was everything. Pretty clothes or fun were not available to her, and she learned very early that you have to work hard to have anything at all.

From the time Grandmother was a little girl, she felt that she was loved only if she could contribute. I mention this only because I know she lived with that feeling from the time she was a child, and only very late in life did she come to a new understanding of being loved just for herself.

The first ten years following Grandfather's death were a new adventure for her since she had devoted herself entirely to making him happy for the forty-four years they had together. It was not that she did not love that role, because she did. However, that season was over now, and a new one was about to begin. Now was the time for just her, and life brought many new and interesting things to do. She was open to it all.

She played golf and bridge with the girls, dated often, volunteered at church, spent time visiting the elderly in nursing homes, attended church regularly, and all in all led a busy and happy life.

Ten years sped quickly by, and she seemed to enjoy them all. We began to recognize, after a series of small strokes, that she was just a bit weaker each day even though the strokes themselves left no telltale signs. It was time for us to talk about what the future might hold for her.

We made a surprise visit for her eightieth birthday, and she was delighted. After a wonderful dinner during which we shared stories about Grandfather and the time they spent with us before he went to heaven, we started to talk.

We danced around the question, trying as hard as we could to be sensitive but getting nowhere. Suddenly Jon, our middle son, said, "Grandmother, picture this! You've had a big stroke, you're walking and talking funny, and you can't live alone anymore. What would you like us to do? These are your options. One, you can stay here in your own home, and you will have live-in help. Two, you can go into a nursing home nearby so your friends can visit you here. Three, you can come and live with us in Jacksonville. What do you think?" By now everyone was laughing at the bluntness of the conversation, letting Grandmother know the advantages and disadvantages of each option. It was a lively exchange all the way around, and when things finally quieted down, she looked at us smiling and simply said, "I'd like to go to Jacksonville and live with all of you, if that ever happens." End of discussion. When the time came for a change, we would know it, and she would come and make her home with us, until she joined Grandfather in heaven.

The call came one afternoon from Sandra, a niece whom she had raised, saying she heard a change in Grandmother's speech and ability to understand. A quick call confirmed her concerns and sent us to south Florida within hours. She was smiling when we arrived, assuring us that she was just fine, happy we had arrived safely, and going right to bed now. Barely two minutes had passed when we heard a loud crash, sending us flying to her room. Grandmother had collapsed on the floor and was only barely responsive when George lifted her gently to the bed. Within a few minutes she was asking what had happened to her, making us wonder just how often this experience had occurred in the past.

Early the next morning we called her doctor to ask about her last visit, since she always said he told her she was doing really well. He advised us that she could no longer live alone safely and agreed to forward her medical records to a friend in Jacksonville, Dr. Arthur Browning, who would look after her with great kindness for the next ten years.

When Grandmother awakened in the morning, we told her of the conversation we had with her physician, and it was amazing to see how willing she was to hear his recommendation that she come to live with us. The ease with which she accepted it told us just how much she had kept to herself and how relieved she was now to be coming home with us. At eighty-two she was starting yet another new adventure in her life.

She often laughed over the years about how she thought she would come to us like Grandfather did, getting comfortable and cared for and going on to heaven in about two or three months' time. That was not to be for Grandmother, and so the next ten years were filled with a new kind of life. It was different and challenging, but in the end one that helped us all to grow in ways we never expected. She brought God's face to us in many new ways along with the opportunity to love as He did, but I would be lying if I said that it was always easy. God tested us all in the fire of this new experience and taught us many things He wanted us to learn through each other.

Since George and I both worked, numerous phone calls throughout the day kept us connected. George's job allowed him to come and go as needed, during which time he would take Grandmother to the grocery store, beauty salon, doctor's appointments, or for a nice lunch, just the two of them. Grandmother cherished these moments alone with her son, and although a great deal of conversation was never overly important to either of them, they enjoyed the quiet together-ness they shared.

Over the next ten years, she continued going to Boston each year for a week to visit Sandra, whom she had raised and loved dearly. Sandra's position in the field of psychology enabled her to help Grandmother become her own person in so many ways after Grandfather's death and contributed greatly to a new understanding of herself.

She looked forward to her time with her daughter, Janet, and her extended family in Illinois and basked in the atten-tion her children, grandchildren, and great-grandchildren gave to her while visiting there.

I often called her from work in the late afternoon, asking if she wanted a "night on the town," and she never said no. We would go out for Chinese or lobster night at a local seafood place, and sometimes she asked to go to the club we belonged to just so she could get more dressed up. We usually ate until we were full and then had them wrap up the rest. More often than not, we drove off with the food still resting on the roof of the car. Gales of laughter could be heard as we saw egg rolls, chicken chow mein, or lobster tails sailing through the air. It was on nights like these that we spoke about feelings, how much we loved her, how happy we were to have her with us, and how much the boys loved knowing she felt safe there. Grandmother did not share her feelings easily most of her life, but as she got older and began to understand how dearly she was loved just for herself, she became really comfortable expressing herself. She always asked how I could love her so much since she was not my mother and had "hung on" so much longer than she thought she would. It was during those times that we laughed and cried together with her, usually saying she had only been with us a year or two, when it was more like seven or eight years, and she would laugh through her tears at the very thought of it.

As things began to change and she was unable to drive to church or to the store, it was important for her to do more things with and for others, even if she was doing them at home. We added steps and a walkway and railing into her beloved garden, where she would spend hours pulling weeds, trimming bushes, and encouraging flowers to grow. Occasionally she could be seen taking a fall straight back, just like Tim Conway did on *The Carol Burnett Show*, with a neighbor calling George or me to let us know. Our neighbors were on the lookout for her whenever she ventured outside these days, and she could hardly believe how fast we could get home to check on her after a fall. She was falling down more these days, and if no one was looking, she simply took herself off to bed for a nap, never mentioning what had happened. She so badly did not want to be a burden that the truth might only come out when we saw a bruise or bump on her head.

By now eight years had passed, and Grandmother's ninetieth birthday was celebrated with as many of her favorite people as could fit around our dining room table. She looked as beautiful as always and basked in the spotlight of her very special day. The slowing-down process was evident in every aspect of her life, and as her weariness grew she would often say to me, "Why do you all still love me so much? I can't do anything for you anymore." I reminded her over and over again that she had been a wonderful mother-in-law to me for more than forty years, and it was a good thing that she was, because loving her and doing for her was so easy for me now. She had been a positive, kind, and loving influence on me, and I was happy she was with us.

The day usually ended with us watching two back-to-back episodes of *The Golden Girls* together, and she would laugh so hard at the things in the old mother's life that she could so easily relate to her own. She especially loved her bawdy little jokes, which she repeated to herself with a chuckle, and I often thought she would love to tell us off on occasion, just as Dorothy's mother did on TV.

When Grandmother was ninety-one, it was clear to us that she was declining, and although she did not have a terminal illness per se, she was simply getting wearier every day. She often said that she thought her time was coming to an end, and she seemed so accepting of that fact and anxious for it to get here. I often saw that both in elderly patients in my care as well as the younger ones who had suffered over a long period of time with chronic illness that was now in a terminal phase. It was not so much that they wanted to die and leave their loved ones as it was a certain sense that they had lived out the life they were given, and they were ready to trade it for a promised new life called eternity.

We knew that we needed the extra help that hospice would provide for Grandmother's care, so we called them one afternoon. They came early the next day and put in place the team of professionals that would love and care for Grandmother and help us in more ways than one can imagine. She loved the nurses, doctors, social workers, and volunteers who visited her at home. She basked in all the new attention for herself, and I know she was grateful that we too were finding comfort in their guidance and counsel.

A monitor in her room kept us ever vigilant at night, and she had only to call our name to have someone at her bedside within seconds. The agreement that she not get up alone without calling was broken one night when our son Ken came running at three in the morning to say Grandmother had fallen on the bathroom floor and was really hurt. We picked her up as easily as we could and, laying her on the bed, began to wash and cover her with clean clothes and warm blankets as she was shivering very hard. A call to her hospice nurse, Dianne, enabled us to have her taken immediately to the hospice center for the night.

It was mid-November now, and Grandmother remained only slightly responsive for six days, during which time we kept her as comfortable as possible. Calls to family and friends brought lots of visiting over the next three weeks, during which time she became more alert and responsive. We treasure many touching memories from those visits. My son George Jr. stayed for several days. The sight of my son Jon kneeling next to her bed is forever etched on my heart.

Everyone took their turn spending private time with her, loving her and thanking her for all she had been to each of them.

Grandmother would ask me many times throughout the day if her room was right next door to my office. It seemed to give her great comfort as I walked in and out all day long. The constancy of everyone's loving attention, to say nothing of the angels in nurses' uniforms who ministered to her, gave her a sweet and gentle peace. Friends from her church came by, often assuring her of God's love for her and singing her sweet hymns. It was all she needed to hear. Ken, our youngest son, needed to be out of town for the weekend. He was concerned that he would not be with Grandmother when she died and had a very tender conversation with her before he left, telling her that she was not to go anywhere until he came back. Ken and Grandmother had a sweet relationship going back to his childhood, and she understood very well what he meant. She smiled when he kissed her good-bye.

Early one morning, I stopped in to see her before going to my office, and Sandra was with her. "Grandmother is telling us something very special this morning," she said, encouraging her to repeat her words for me.

"The tail boat is here, dear," she said, quietly smiling.

"You mean the sailboat?" I asked.

"No, I mean the tail boat. Don't you know what the tail boat is?"

"Are you going to get on the tail boat now?" I asked.

"Not yet," she said. "Number seven, eight, and nine are ahead of me."

"How will you know when it's your turn?" I asked.

"Oh, they are very nice here, dear, they come for you," she answered softly, just as if she were talking about any other natural thing around her. Grandmother was not a very verbal person by nature or given to emotional or lengthy conversation. Here she was now, explaining to us in very happy tones that the tail boat was in the harbor waiting for her, but others were going to be taken first, and when it was her turn they would let her know and come for her. She said all this with a very sweet smile on her face, fully at peace with everyone and everything around her and totally unafraid.

Grandmother's experience of journeying to America by boat at two years old may have played a role in the imagery she was now experiencing of going on this, her final journey. The "tail boat" of which she was speaking would take her on this new journey now, to the heaven she was certain was awaiting her.

She died the next evening, just as Ken came into her room and whispered in her ear that he was home again. There is no doubt in my mind that she knew he was there, as he had promised. At the end of her earthly life, she was surrounded by the family who loved her dearly. She understood finally that she was loved totally for herself and not for what she could contribute or do for others. I am certain all of heaven was happy to see her.

All of life is a journey from the day we are born until the day we die. We are learning every minute we are alive. No one, except the God who made us, knows what He put into each of our baskets of learning when we were conceived in our mother's womb. Only He knows the process by which we will grow to spiritual maturity and how easy or how hard the lessons will be for us. He will provide all the nourishment required to complete the journey well, but we have to be willing to learn from each and every person He puts on the path to teach us, whether or not we think the person is worthy of that role. In so doing, the underneath-threads, subtly woven by Him, will complete the tapestry of our lives, unseen by us.

Grandmother allowed God to teach her what He wanted her to learn while she was with us those ten years and to use her to grow us, as individuals, into the family He wanted us to become. We are forever grateful to her for being His willing vessel for our refining.

# Mommy

*"George, take me to John now, please."*

Margaret Mary Fitzpatrick was two years old when her mother died of tuberculosis, and she found no permanent home until her father remarried when she was seven. Until that time, she lived with maiden aunts or cousins, and later in a boarding house, where her father visited her nightly on his way home from work. She wondered why the sound of concert music made her cry deep inside her soul. It wasn't until years later that she learned her mother played classical piano every day, and one day the music simply stopped. The yearning for love and a sense of belonging did not find a soft and safe place to rest until she met my father.

As different as night is from day, Margaret Mary, known as Peggy Fitzpatrick, and John Joseph Patrick Horan were married in 1935. Together they raised four daughters with very little money, lots of hard work and determination, unfailing love, and constant prayer. They walked the mile to mass rain or shine each morning, in a tiny town called Tappan, New

York. Some of our fondest memories are of them pulling us to church on Sundays on a toboggan sled in the snow, a rope tied around both their waists.

When Dad died in 1973, Mom was only sixty-five years old and had many very productive years ahead of her, during which time she traveled extensively and worked for the church in one capacity or another well into her eighties. She read her cherished books, taught herself to play more than 150 songs on the organ, and loved her children and grandchildren dearly. I can still picture her driving the forty-five minutes from her house to mine, windows down, white hair blowing in the breeze, all the while her beloved classical music playing on the radio for all the world to hear. She was fun, disciplined, tender, pretty, strongly determined, opinionated, ever prayerful, dependent on love, and she touched everyone she met with both her humanity and her deeply spiritual soul.

Maureen, the oldest of my sisters, lived with Mom before Dad died and continued to until Mom was almost ninety. By then it was getting harder for Mom to be alone all day while Maureen worked, so she spent two or three days a week with Peg, or Maggie as she was called, who lived nearby. Mom loved being with Peg and Jim, who had a special room decorated beautifully just for her. "You are wonderful," she would say to them as they waited on her hand and foot, treating her like a queen and serving her the sweets she loved so much, while making her laugh at just about everything. Over the years Mom and Peg forged a very deep, mutually respectful, and abiding friendship. It allowed them to love completely and without reserve. Fiercely independent all her life, Mom continued to want to be so, even as she was becoming frailer, and she insisted on going back to her own home after a few days away.

Anne visited from New Jersey regularly, bringing her own very special brand of tenderness. As the youngest in the family, Anne had always been the helper, the one who tried to make everything right, and the one who would give you the shirt she was wearing if you needed it. Now she was trying so hard, despite all the truths of what was happening to Mom, to make her well so she would not go away. She wanted her to be here forever, and she thought just wanting could make it so. It was not to be, and I think the loss of Mom was hardest on Anne, as the baby of the family, since this time she just couldn't make it all better. She filled Mom's life with herbal teas, delicious hand and body lotions, exercises she felt would keep her limber, any vitamin she thought would make her strong, lovely dresses, shawls, and jackets to keep her cozy and warm, and hugs and kisses at every turn in the road.

Maureen filled her life with the news of each working day. The comings and goings of people she worked with, and all the high jinks she could share with great humor and flair. They looked back on happy and wonderful vacations they shared, especially the one to Czechoslovakia, where Mom had wanted to go all her life. For her, that trip was the culmination of a lifelong dream, and she often expressed the sheer joy of sharing it with Maureen. Maureen stayed awake each night until Mom used the bathroom for the last time and listened for her all through the night to make sure she was safe and secure. Maureen loved her as only a first daughter can, and Mom knew that so well.

But it was September now, and Mom was in her ninety-first year. She was tired and not wanting to go back and forth anymore. And so it was that she came to me for her final year on earth. She and I had been more like sisters than mother and daughter, for some reason that only God knew about. We had relied on and counseled each other the way you do with a very close friend from the time I was a young girl. The trust we shared was the cornerstone of our lifelong friendship. Mom had said many times over the years, "When it's my time, I will come and stay with you, OK?" Thus it was that she spent the last year of life nestled with me and my family, comfortably at peace, meditating on the life of Christ, listening to the wonderful classical music she loved, watching George Will on the nightly news, sitting on the patio overlooking the lake, and visited by her children, grandchildren, and a myriad of friends who loved her dearly.

One day out of the blue, I asked her if she could give me just one word for her whole life, and without hesitating she replied, smiling, "Fantastic!" She had fought the good fight, grown by God's grace, and now saw life as "fantastic." Many a day sitting quietly, she would simply smile and say to me, "It's very peaceful here, dear. I'm so grateful and happy to be with you. Love you so much, you know." A million dollars could not replace this precious time together.

Her September birthday was celebrated with only those closest to her, since she never liked drawing attention to herself, and that did not change now. The holidays came and went quietly, and each day found her looking more and more forward to going to heaven to see her beloved John again. "Have you and I talked about everything we need to now?" she said one afternoon. "Is everything settled with my house, and is everything in order for the girls?" This was a mother who had counted out the exact same number of presents for each of her children every Christmas morning, so it would be fair all the way around. She was doing it now, wanting everything to be perfect for all her girls.

Spring brought warm sunny days, lots of napping time, her lovely classical music, communion often, and prayers all day long. She loved her rainbow sherbet, scrambled eggs and bacon in tiny amounts, and chicken soup, although she told me once that if I gave her any more she was sure she would grow feathers. Friends came by to give her a manicure, to trim and shampoo her hair, to listen to music with her, to look at old photographs, and to hear the stories she had to share behind each one.

She spoke often about her father and how good he had been to her, and how happy she would be to see him again. Although he had died when she was only twenty-five, her memories of him were vivid and full of love and devotion. "Someone is calling, 'Margaret, Margaret,'" she said to me one day, smiling. "I think it's Papa or maybe Aunt Margaret. I think they want to see me." She said this very naturally, the way those who are getting close to their dying time always do. She often spoke about the mother she longed for and missed all her life, and quietly called out, "Mama, Mama," from time to time. She wondered if she would recognize her, since she was only two years old when her mother had died and did not really remember her. I promised her that in some way that only God could arrange, she would recognize her mother's face as soon as she saw her, and I believe that is truly what happened one very special day before she died.

April was a turning point in Mom's condition, as she was weaker in every way and asking more often when I thought God would take her into heaven. She wanted to find the "bridegroom," she said. "I just want to sit at the Master's feet and be with Him now. I have no more longing for this life. Where is the door to heaven? Can I get up and go in now?"

"No, Mom, your angel will come for you here and take you to heaven from this room when it is time," I said.

She seemed so contented to know it would happen that way, and smiling she said to me, "Your father would be so proud of you, dear."

One of the sweetest experiences she had during this time was a visit from Doctor George Joseph, a physician she was very fond of and on whom she relied greatly. He quietly prayed with her the simple and familiar prayers she knew so well, reading them from a small prayer book from his childhood. It would be hard to describe the sheer joy and comfort this single act of kindness brought to her. When he gave her a fatherly permission to "go on" any time she felt she was ready, it was so much more than what it seemed. It was as if her own father was giving her permission to go home, and she was so happy to hear that from him. How good God was to comfort her through the very person He knew she would see as an authority figure and who could touch her soul in just this way.

As spring made way for summer, Anne visited often, and Peggy came three days a week to tend to Mom's every need. She loved three of my closest friends dearly, and Edry, Lenora, and Jackie loved her back. All three were an enormous comfort to her, stopping by for visits, bringing her beautiful flowers, listening to her lovely music, and just sitting quietly holding her hand. Maureen visited on her days off, and nightly calls were the norm. By now I was working at home most mornings, with a special friend staying with Mom until I got home from work on days that Peg or Anne were not here. George was very good at getting Mom up and into the recliner, taking her to the bathroom, quenching her thirst, and making her comfortable. Since his office is at home, he was available most of the time, and some of my most tender memories are of him gently meeting whatever need she expressed to him. "George, take me to John now, please," she pleaded one day as he was lifting her back in bed. She saw him as someone in charge who could arrange things, and her heart-stopping request was answered with his quiet and understanding smile as he reassured her that he had heard her request and that she would see her beloved John soon.

By now, the intimate and interior conversations she'd had with Jesus all her life became vocal. "Jesus, come and take me to heaven with You," she pleaded often. "I have no more longing for this life. I want to give my heart to You. Be my strength. I love You. I can't do this alone." For Mom, intimate conversations like this with the Jesus she loved so much came very naturally. He had been her savior, redeemer, lover, sanctifier, brother, and friend throughout her life, and that did not change now. Her conversations and pleadings with Him were so personal and touching to hear and made the presence of the Lord she loved extraordinarily real and a wonderful gift to those of us close enough to hear.

"Who is the old man standing in the corner looking at me?" she asked one day while I was sitting in bed with her. "He is dressed all in white, and he is just watching me." Patients so often speak of angels that stay near to them at this stage in their lives and almost always describe them as eight feet tall, male, with gowns so white they appear luminous. "Do you think it's your angel?" I asked. She nodded. When I said, "It would be just like you to get an old angel," she smiled and said, "You are my heart. I'm so glad I had you." There are no words to describe the tenderness and love reflected in both her voice and her beautiful sky-blue eyes at moments like this.

Hospice care at this time made an enormous difference for Mom and helped us in a very real and tangible way to prepare for this last phase in her long and meaningful life. When healing and recovery are no longer possible and dying is inevitable, hospice care enables the person to live life to the fullest, pain free, in physical, emotional, and spiritual comfort, until there are no more days left. Nancy, Barbara, and Dianne were Mom's hospice angels and cared for and loved her as no three other professionals could. "Life is so heavy in my chest now, I can't hold on any longer, please help me," she said one day. "I'm running out of time and space, will you release me, dear, and let me go?"

Mom was so close to her dying time now, and most days were filled with bathing and turning her, keeping her out of pain, putting cool cloths to her forehead and ice chips to her lips, and sleeping with her each night, arms around each other. Her eyes remained open almost all of the time, and she seemed to be peacefully looking all around the room. Maureen came for a visit on Mom's last day with us, giving her permission to die and encouraging her to go on to the God she loved so much. It seemed to be just what she was waiting for. For Mom, the assurance that her oldest child was in her own home for the first time, safe and secure and living close to her sisters, was all-important.

When we die, our body separates itself from our soul, and it is this separation that people often explain to you in minute detail, if you will listen to them. This is when they tell you about seeing angels or loved ones who have died before them or hearing beautiful choirs of angelic voices. They seem to have the experience of traveling back and forth between earth and heaven and have often been heard to say in whispered voices, "I'm in a waiting place; it's very nice here. I am not with you anymore, but I'm not in heaven yet either." If you let them know that everything they are experiencing is normal and natural to their journey, they take that final step into the eternity that God has promised them since the beginning of time, totally unafraid and at peace.

So it was for Mom on that last day. My mother had a deep and abiding devotion to Jesus all her life, so I placed a statue of Him on the side table next to her bed and repeated the prayers she loved the most. Turning her from side to side hourly, I simply placed the statue on the left, then the right of the bed for her to see. She never closed her eyes once on that final day, and I encouraged her to rest her weary head on His heart and just let Him hold her, assuring her that she would find comfort and safety there and be with Him safely in heaven that day. The hour was late, and Lenora and Joe, who had spent the evening with us, were getting ready to go home. Lenora quietly slipped into Mom's room and kissed her gently good-bye. Mom loved her dearly, and I was so grateful to have her here with me now and for her to be the last one to kiss Mom good-bye.

I knew that Mom's time was growing very short, so I slipped into bed with her and, wrapping my arms around her, held her close to my heart. "You are going into heaven now," I said to her, "and I will stay with you until you are safely there, just like we always promised. Daddy will be the first one you see at the head of the line. He will have a baseball bat in his hands, knocking everyone else out of the way, because you know he never wanted anyone closer to you than he was."

Lying very quietly with her head resting on mine, she simply smiled, closed her eyes, and died. We stayed nestled together that way for a long, long time. She was safe now in the loving arms of the God she had loved and trusted all her life, with her beloved John beside her. It does not get any better than this, and I will be forever grateful to her and to God for allowing me the honor of loving her until the end.

Mom's entire life was a life of faith. She spread the gift she had been given everywhere she went and loved her God more intimately than anyone else I have ever known. She sought Him out in all the painful spaces of her growing-up years and recognized Him in the many people He sent to journey with her. In spite of the enormous hole left in her heart by her mother's death, she learned to reach out and gently comfort others who were in need. She had an especially tender heart for children when they were hurt or lost, and would always jump to the aid of the underdog or someone who was frightened by the circumstances of life. She allowed the grace of God, sent her way through the powerful prayers of her parents, to grow her into the person she was meant to become. She was one of a kind, and I know that Daddy is glad to have her back with him now.

# Conclusion

Everyone dies.

Sooner or later every life that has come into being, whether it is a very long life or a short one, will end. Before we experience our own death, the likelihood that each one of us will be with a loved one or friend as they are dying is great. The stories, conversations, and experiences real people share with us paint a canvas we are all anxious to understand and learn from. In listening closely to the stories, death and the process of dying are taken out of the context of the physical and brought into the context of the spiritual as the soul journeys back to its Creator. God's hand can clearly be seen in every story regardless of the past spirituality of the individual person or their family members. He offers meaning, hope, comfort, and understanding to those whose earthly life is ending. At the end of their lives people often explain in very tender tones that it is all about "love"—nothing more, nothing less.

They are aware of being accompanied by an all-loving presence that allows them to review their lives, seeing clearly the opportunities presented to them and the choices they made. The reviewing time so many people speak of never seems to be a time of scorn or fear but rather an opportunity to see and understand things from God's perspective. In dying they seem to be experiencing the insights and ultimate healing of God's unconditional love.

As in all experiences of life, there are two sides to every coin. In preparing to welcome each of His children home to Himself, God is teaching those around that person the lessons He knows they need to learn the most. In these shared experiences, God teaches them each something different while they are caring for a loved one or friend who is dying. They often say afterward that they knew the lessons were from God because they were not ones they would necessarily have chosen to learn on their own.

People frequently have asked me, "What is the most important thing you have learned over the last thirty-two years of caring for friends, family members, and patients who were terminally ill and dying?" My answer, without hesitation, is now and always has been that God simply loves each and every person He has ever created, warts and all. It is His wish that not one be lost. The extent to which He will go to make this happen is awesome to see and touch and feel. It is palpable in all the experiences God allows His children to have as He is preparing to take them home to Himself.

Dying is a very natural part of living. It is not an ending but a beginning. A transition into the life God has promised to all of His children. He wants us home with Him when we finish the work He created us to do. He loves us—believe it.

# Acknowledgments

To my husband, George, whose unselfish love and constant encouragement and support made the writing of this book possible.

And to our sons, George Jr., Jon Hugh, Kenneth David, and Erik, for their patience, good humor, and faith that enabled me to complete this manuscript.

In loving memory of my parents, Peggy and John Horan, whose example laid the spiritual and moral foundation for our family and the work we were to do in our lives.

To Sister Naureen Marie, whose beautiful and gentle spirit taught me that the nurse at the bedside is invaluable in the true healing of God's children.

I gratefully acknowledge the earliest pioneers of end-of-life hospice care who recognized the need for a more personal and supportive way to serve the needs of those whose lives were limited in time by a terminal illness. They set about to create an environment of spiritual, emotional, and physical comfort and well-being in a way that had not yet found its place in the medical community. We owe a great debt of gratitude to them for the strides made, against all odds, in creating and teaching a new way for people to live to the fullest each day, until there are no more tomorrows left to them. Their names are too numerous to mention here but include Dame Cicely Saunders, Joy Ufema, and Elizabeth Kübler-Ross. Their determination on a national and international level moved the understanding of end-of-life care to the noble place it holds today.

Paul Brenner, Dottie Dorion, Gene Lewis, Phaon and Kay Derr, Lois Graessle, Dr. Matt Becker, Gretchen Bell, Jack Galliard, Shirley Doyle, Linda Brown, Billye Boselli, Dr. George Wilson, Dr. Fred Schert, Dr. Max Karrer, Dr. Sam Day, Jeanne Christie, Betty Hurtz, and many others played a major role in founding the hospice program with which I was associated for more than twenty-two years.

The nurses, chaplains, social workers, home health aides, and laypeople were the heart and soul of the tiny hospice program and received such little compensation as to be considered a stipend rather than a salary. Without their commitment, perseverance, and compassion, patients would not have received the tender loving care that enabled them to die with peace and dignity. These hospice workers know well who they are, and they can bask quietly in the knowledge that their noble work has made an enormous contribution to the living and dying time of thousands of patients and families for more than twenty-five years.

Special thanks to Jackie Aquino, RN, who started this journey with me more than twenty-five years ago and to Edry Rowe Surrency for her devotion and dedication, which made this work possible.

Special recognition to dear friends Guy Cuddihee, Patti Hendricks Joyce, and Melody Simmons for their untiring enthusiasm for the telling of the stories in this book.

Carol Susan Roth, my agent, was tireless in her efforts to bring this book to public awareness and understanding. She enthusiastically represented me in all the best ways possible and provided encouragement every step of the way.

**Trudy Harris, RN**, was a hospice nurse for many years, moving on to become president of the Hospice Foundation for Caring. During those 22 years she continued to play a very natural role for her as a nurse, in helping people to enter the hospice program when she knew it would be helpful and appropriate for them to do so. At the same time Harris took on additional roles in marketing, public relations, fund-raising, and development, raising more than 45 million dollars in capital contributions for the HFC. These successes enabled the organization to establish a residential care facility for 24 patients and an in-patient facility within a local teaching hospital for 28 patients, to obtain property for a third facility for patient care, and to create an Educational Institute through which physicians, nurses, social workers, and other medical professionals are trained in the understanding of end-of-life and hospice care. She was hired by the local hospice when it was serving 6 to 10 patients a day and retired when it was serving 950 terminally ill and dying patients every day. She retired feeling that the work to which God had drawn her many years before had been accomplished. She is now retired and living in Jacksonville, Florida, with her husband and enjoys traveling, being with friends, and loving her four grandchildren.